His Way

by Jack Cottrell

You may obtain a 64-page leader's guide to accompany this paperback. Order number 40080 from Standard Publishing or your local supplier.

A Division of Standard Publishing
Cincinnati, Ohio 45231
No. 40079

Table of Contents

1 Living Under Law   3

2 God Is Supreme   11

3 No Graven Images   18

4 God's Holy Name   26

5 Lord of Time   34

6 Human Authority   41

7 Respect for Human Life   47

8 Marriage and Sex   53

9 Steal No More   60

10 Truth Is Basic   66

11 The Peril of Greed   72

12 The Greatest Commandment   77

13 Love in Action   83

14 The Highest Good   89

Bible quotations are from the King James Version except when another version is indicated by one of the following abbreviations:

NAS—New American Standard Version © 1971 by the Lockman Foundation

ASV—American Standard Version of 1901

© 1979, the STANDARD PUBLISHING Company, a division of STANDEX INTERNATIONAL CORPORATION.

Library of Congress Catalog No. 78-62710
ISBN 0-87239-238-4

Printed in U.S.A.   1979

1

Living Under Law

Basic Scripture resources: Exodus 20:1, 2
Deuteronomy 5:32—6:3; Psalm 119:97-104;
Matthew 5:17; Mark 12:13-17

The present generation has witnessed an unprecedented assault upon the very concept of law. For many people the phrase *law and order* has become an expression of contempt. Radical theologians and advocates of the "new morality" keep telling us that the human race has "come of age," meaning that it has reached a level of moral maturity that should enable it to get along without laws.

Such rebellion against law should not surprise us, for the Bible says the very essence of sin is lawlessness (1 John 3:4, NAS). A spirit of lawlessness has been in the world almost from the beginning. The apostle Paul testified to its presence in his day, and he indicated that it would get much worse before the end (2 Thessalonians 2:3-8, NAS).

In the face of such lawlessness the Christian must continue to uphold the sanctity and validity of law, both human and divine. The Christian teacher must be able to meet the challenge of the anarchists in his classroom. Christian parents especially must be able to convey to their children a sound rationale and a deep respect for law, both by explanation and by example.

It is true, of course, that we are not under law but are under grace (Romans 6:14). This means that we are not under a law code as a way of salvation. We are not saved by law, but by grace. It does *not* mean, however, that a Christian under grace is no longer obligated to obey the laws that apply in our age. Even though we are not under law as a standard to be *judged* by, we definitely are under law as a standard to *live* by.

In this opening chapter we will give a brief explanation of what it means to live under law. We will discuss the basis, the source, and the nature of law.

1. The Basis of Law

The basic rationale for the validity of law is the fact that we live in a God-created universe. The world in which we live did not originate by blind chance. It did not develop into its present state according to the impersonal forces of naturalistic evolution. This universe was planned and created by God (Genesis 1:1).

A God of Order

Who is this God who has created the heavens and the earth? Is He an irrational being who does things in a disorderly, disorganized way? Hardly. When Paul was instructing the Corinthians to conduct their church affairs "decently and in order" (1 Corinthians 14:40), he suggested this is only proper since "God is not the author of confusion" (1 Corinthians 14:33).

That God is "not the author of confusion" is important not only for the kind of worship services we ought to have, but also for the kind of universe we actually live in. It is a God-created universe, and therefore an orderly universe, a universe that operates according to law.

God has built "law and order" into the very structure of creation. Nowhere is this more obvious than in the realm of natural law. The movements of stars and planets and their satellites are so beautifully regular that they are the most exact indicators "for signs, and

4

for seasons, and for days, and years" (Genesis 1:14). The Creator has established laws of genetics whereby each category of living things reproduces after its kind (Genesis 1:11, 12, 21, 24, 25).

The Moral Law

Just as God has made natural law an inherent part of His orderly creation in general, so also has He built His moral law into the fabric of human nature in particular. Why does every human creature on the face of the earth have a set of laws and regulations and taboos? Why is there such a remarkable agreement among these law codes with regard to their general emphasis against such things as adultery, theft, and murder? It is because God has created mankind with a built-in awareness of the rightness and wrongness of certain things. Thus Paul can say that even those people who have never seen the specially-revealed law of God (the Bible), may nevertheless "do by nature the things contained in the law," and thereby "show the work of the law written in their hearts" (Romans 2:14, 15).

God wrote this law on the hearts of men when He created mankind in His own image (Genesis 1:26). Unfortunately sin has defaced the image-character in us, thereby dimming our awareness of the moral law and requiring a radical renewal process before it can be useful again. This renewal of the image of God in us is one of the fruits of conversion to Christ, which is described in effect as a re-creation in God's image (see Ephesians 4:20-24; Colossians 3:9, 10).

The restoration of the sin-marred image involves being re-created "in righteousness and true holiness" (Ephesians 4:24) and being "renewed in knowledge" (Colossians 3:10).

What is this moral law that God has stamped upon the very heart of His crowning creature, man? It does not include all the various laws that God has given from time to time and that apply only to a limited time or place, such as the laws of sacrifice and temple worship. These applied only to the Jewish nation in the Old Testament era. The term *moral law* refers rather to those moral principles that are universally and eternally valid, those that apply to all men in all times. These include the laws requiring love and truth and justice. These are the laws that reflect the very nature of God himself (see Matthew 5:44, 45; 1 Peter 1:16; 1 John 4:8, 16).

Civil Government

Even human laws, the laws imposed upon citizens by civil authorities, should ideally be nothing more than an extension of the divine moral law. God himself has ordained the existence of civil government so that it may enact and enforce law. Paul says that "the powers that be are ordained of God" (Romans 13:1). He describes the role of civil authorities:

> For rulers are not a terror to good works, but to the evil. Wilt thou then not be afraid of the power? do that which is good, and thou shalt have praise of the same: for he is the minister of God to thee for good. But if thou do that which is evil, be afraid; for he beareth not the sword in vain: for he is the minister of God, a revenger to execute wrath upon him that doeth evil (Romans 13:3, 4).

There is a strong emphasis here on good and evil. The civil government encourages good works and punishes evil works. It must do this by establishing and enforcing laws. Who will decide what is good and what is evil? Are rulers and lawmakers free to decide this as they please? No! Ideally they are God's ministers and should look to Him and to His eternal moral law as the ultimate standard. When governments are operating according to their God-given roles, they will be making and enforcing laws that are in accord with God's moral law.

Why, then, is there law? The answer is that it just could not be any other way, since this is a God-created universe. The God who made the worlds is a God of reason and order. He created the human race in His own image, which means that His moral law is imprinted on the hearts of all. He ordained civil government to maintain "law and order" in accord with His moral law.

II. The Source of Law

Since law is so important for an orderly, peaceful society and for a life that is pleasing to God, it is obviously essential that we have a knowledge of this law. But how can we know it?

We have already suggested that any innate knowledge of right and wrong has been spoiled by sin, and that the renewal of this knowledge comes only with conversion to Christ. But how is this accomplished? Does it come automatically at Christian baptism? Is new knowledge of God's law simply implanted directly in the heart? The answer is no. Once the original creation knowledge has been defaced, it can be renewed only through a study of the revelation that God has given us in the Bible.

This means that we do not have a *subjective* source of law. We do not have a reliable inner moral sense. The only source of law that we can trust is the *objective* Word of God. To this alone can we turn for a true knowledge of right and wrong.

There are several false ideas regarding the source of law. One is that the conscience is a reliable moral guide. "Let your conscience be your guide," is the popular philosophy. This is a serious misunderstanding of the function of the conscience. The conscience is not a built-in source of information about right and wrong. Rather, it presupposes that such knoweldge is already present. Then, like a moral alarm system, it merely *compares* an action with one's accepted ideas of what is right and wrong. If the act is one already determined to be wrong, the conscience "hurts" or accuses us or makes us feel guilty when we commit such an act.

In this sense the conscience is like a computer, which can sort data correctly *only* if it has been programmed accurately. The computer will perform its functions faithfully even if programmed improperly, but its results will be unreliable. Likewise the conscience will operate with whatever value system a person has accepted; it will continue to "accuse or excuse" with regard to particular acts. But if the accepted value system happens to be the wrong one, the conscience will accuse and excuse the wrong things.

In other words, the conscience itself is not a guide: it *needs* a guide. It needs to be taught and informed from some reliable outside source. What is that source? The Bible alone.

Another false idea regarding the source of law is that the Holy Spirit will provide inner guidance in the making of ethical decisions. "Just let the Spirit lead you," is the idea. We must emphatically point out, however, that this is *not* the purpose of the Holy Spirit's presence in the life of the Christian. The Spirit is not given to provide us with inner knowledge. John 16:13 ("He will guide you into all truth") applies only to the apostles. Christians receive the Holy Spirit for quite a different purpose, namely, to give us inner *strength* to do God's will (Ephesians 3:16; Romans 8:13). Our *knowledge* of that will comes only through a study of His Word.

8

As long as we continue to look within ourselves for a knowledge of God's law, we will keep coming up with conflicting and confusing and inadequate answers to life's problems. When we look to God's revelation in the pages of Scripture, and point others to the same source, we will find a law that will bring peace and happiness to ourselves and to society, if everyone will abide by it.

III. The Nature of Law

We live under our Creator's laws, which are revealed to us in the words of the Bible. These laws are just and good, and are designed for the welfare of individuals and of society as a whole.

One thing in particular needs to be stressed concerning the nature of God's laws, especially the eternal moral law that applies in every age. It is this: God's laws are usually general in nature, and require honest and sincere application to the *particular* situations of our lives.

God could have given us a lawbook that spelled out detailed rules and regulations for every possible ethical situation and decision. Of course, if He did this for us—twentieth century Americans—he would have to do it for *all* cultures in *all* times. Can you imagine the size of the library of books that would be required for such detailed instructions? Can you imagine the difficulty of trying to read and understand all those volumes?

This is part of the very genius of the Bible. Here in one small volume, carried in one hand or pocket, are all the laws needed to govern the conduct of all peoples of all times! How is this possible? It is possible because the laws are mostly so general that they transcend cultural differences, and can be given relevant applications from culture to culture, from age to age.

This means that if we are going to use the Bible as God intends, we must know the general laws and principles it teaches and must make every honest effort to see how they apply to particular problems in our lives. A general commandment such as "Be kind to one another" (Ephesians 4:32, NAS), or a general principle such as "Blessed are the meek" (Matthew 5:5) binds us to particular forms of conduct that we can know by serious study and meditation.

If the Bible does not mention a particular issue by name, such as cigarette smoking or labor strikes, that does not mean it is silent on these problems. There are general principles that do apply, and it is wrong for us not to apply them.

In the following chapters we will be studying many of the great general commandments and principles of God's law. We will try to understand the principles themselves, and we will see how they apply to many particular moral problems in our time. There are other principles and other applications, which the readers are urged to investigate for themselves.

2

God Is Supreme

*Basis Scripture resources: Exodus 20:3
Matthew 6:24-34; James 4:7, 8*

Each of the Ten Commandments is an ethical application of a general doctrinal truth. The first Commandment is "Thou shalt have no other gods before me." The general principle that underlies it is the absolute and exclusive lordship of God.

The goal of this chapter is to explore the meaning and implications of the first Commandment. What does it mean to let God be supreme in one's life? What attitudes and practices are ruled out for those who truly have no others before God?

I. Ultimate Authority

It is no accident that the command, "Thou shalt have no other gods before me," is first among the Ten Commandments. This is the command that deals with ultimate authority, and this is the question that must be settled first of all. Who is going to have the final say, the final word in our lives? Who is going to determine what is truth? Who is going to make the decisions concerning right and wrong? Who is going to determine how we spend our time and money? This Commandment requires that it be God. It is useless to consider any of the other claims and commandments of Scripture unless we grant that God and God alone has this kind of authority over us.

Everyone must answer these questions. Many people do so quite unconsciously, not realizing the nature of their commitment to a particular god. But it is much better to face these questions deliberately.

Having a God

The question of ultimate authority is bound up in the idea of "having a god." What does it mean to "have a god"? Is it like having a mother? Not exactly. It is more like having a wife or husband. To have a wife or husband, one must make an active and personal choice, and he must yield absolute, exclusive commitment to that individual.

"Having a god" involves such a choice and such a commitment. One yields himself in total submission by personal choice to some person, thing, or idea. Lip-service is not decisive. One's god is that to which he gives supreme devotion, that which ultimately determines his decisions.

One God at a Time

It is impossible to have more than one god at any given time. There can be only one ultimate, one supreme authority. Thus "having a god" is necessarily exclusive, again like having a wife or a husband. Polytheism technically is a belief in more than one god. But even a "polytheist" must have a single supreme principle that rules his life. There will always be one thing that is chosen first and surrendered last, one thing that is the supreme value in a person's life. This is one's god.

Jesus teaches us this truth when He declares that "no man can serve two masters" (Matthew 6:24). Paul reaffirms it when he says, "Ye cannot drink the cup of the Lord, and the cup of devils: ye cannot be partakers of the Lord's table, and of the table of devils" (1 Corinthians 10:21).

12

II. False Gods

Once we understand what it means to have a god, it should be clear that it is impossible not to have a god. Everyone's life is ultimately determined by some supreme value or source of authority, whether he is conscious of it or not. It may not be the true God, the God of the Bible; but nevertheless it is a god.

Many false gods clamor for man's allegiance. These may be easily recognized when they are a part of a formal religion such as Hinduism. The gods that entice twentieth-century western man are much more subtle, however. A father can become so devoted to his family that his sole purpose in life is to give them every possible pleasure and comfort and benefit. On the other hand, a person can become so engrossed with his job or profession that he neglects his responsibility to both God and his family. Many people make science their god when they count it as the supreme authority in the area of truth and knowledge. Anthony Standen has analyzed this false religion in his book, *Science Is a Sacred Cow.*

The Occult

More and more people seem to be turning to occult practices, and those who do are surrendering themselves to false gods. Witchcraft and the "black arts" in general rely upon the power of Satan and are a deliberate renunciation of the true God. Satanism likewise honors the devil as god. Anton LaVey, founder of the Church of Satan of San Francisco, wrote *The Satanic Bible,* in which he pictures Satan as saying, "I am the Lord, your God" (p. 180). (Mr. LaVey himself does not believe there is a real devil; for him "Satan" is merely a personification of what he feels is man's true nature.)

Astrology also exalts a false and alien power above the power of God and is therefore a violation of the first Commandment. The horoscope is a substitute for

13

God and His Word. As one writer has truly observed, astrology is idolatry.

Drug Addiction

The person who has become addicted to a drug has made that drug his god. He has one great desire: to acquire that drug. The drug is supreme. Research indicates that even marijuana creates a psychological addiction that takes control of the user. Every cigarette smoker who has tried to break the habit, whether he has been successful or not, will testify to the addicting power of tobacco. Every alcoholic will confirm the same for alcoholic beverages.

In other words, whenever a person becomes addicted, whether physically or psychologically, to one of these drugs, it becomes a false deity. The first of the Ten Commandments tells us to avoid this.

Mammon

In Matthew 6:24 Jesus singles out mammon as a chief rival for God's throne. *Mammon* is a term that means money or riches. In the latter part of Matthew 6 Jesus condemns those whose main concern in life is to acquire money, or more specifically, the things that money can buy. They serve a false god.

The Self

Perhaps the most sinister of all the false gods is the self. A man is guilty of self-worship when he lets the course of his life be determined by his own desires and preferences, when he sets himself up as the final authority for what is right and wrong, true and false. Modern man calls this *freedom* and demands it: the Bible calls it *idolatry* and condemns it. Philippians 3:19 speaks against those "whose god is their belly," namely, those for whom personal pleasure or happiness is the highest goal.

III. The One True God

The God that we worship must be the true and living God, the God revealed to us in the Bible. Our God rightfully demands exclusive devotion. All His rivals are truly "nothings," or false gods devoid of inherent power and authorityand being. (Psalm 96:5 says that "all the gods of the nations are idols," a word that literally means "nothings.")

No Other Gods

God says we must have no other gods "before" Him. A better translation of this last phrase is "besides" Him: we must have no other gods besides Him or in addition to Him. Jesus repeats this timeless requirement in Matthew 4:10, "Thou shalt worship the Lord thy God, and him only shalt thou serve." The first and greatest commandment likewise guards the absolute and exclusive lordship of God: "Thou shalt love the Lord thy God with all thy heart, and with all thy soul, and with all thy mind" (Matthew 22:37). When Jesus says God is to be loved with *all* the heart and soul and mind, this leaves room for not a single iota of devotion towards another god.

Jesus also says, "Seek ye first the kingdom of God, and his righteousness" (Matthew 6:33). Here again He is saying that we must make God the supreme authority in our lives.

A Rightful Claim

When God first made this demand of Israel following the exodus from Egypt, He reminded them of who He is and what He had done: "I am the Lord thy God, which have brought thee out of the land of Egypt, out of the house of bondage" (Exodus 20:2). He had just demonstrated to the world His absolute and exclusive lordship by marvelously delivering His people from slavery.

The ten plagues that preceded the exodus were calculated to show that God is supreme and that the Egyptian deities were indeed "nothings." Each plague was directed against an area or object that was considered sacred by the Egyptians, such as the Nile River, cattle, the sun, and Pharaoh himself.

It was the Lord God who unmasked these false gods! It was the Lord God who opened the Red Sea for Israel's escape! It was the Lord God who brought them out of the land of Egypt! No wonder He can rightfully demand, "Thou shalt have no other gods besides me."

Surrender to Christ

The God who spoke to Israel following the exodus is the same God who has revealed himself more fully in the New Testament age as God the Father, God the Son, and God the Holy Spirit (see Matthew 28:19 and 2 Corinthians 13:14). In view of this New Testament revelation we cannot obey the first of the Ten Commandments unless our worship is consciously directed to "God in three persons."

More specifically the first Commandment, when applied in the New Testament age, lays down the absolute requirement for being a Christian. We cannot ignore the claims of Jesus Christ and be fully submitted to the true God at the same time. Jesus said, "He that honoreth not the Son honoreth not the Father which hath sent him" (John 5:23). Paul says that "every tongue should confess that Jesus Christ is Lord, to the glory of God the Father" (Philippians 2:11). How can one hope to glorify God if he refuses to accept Jesus as his Lord?

There are many people who say, "I don't need to be a Christian. I keep the Ten Commandments, and that's all God expects of me." But the point is that a person cannot keep even the first of the Ten Commandments unless he is in fact a Christian. (Of course, we accept

16

Christ as Savior and Lord not just because we are required to do so, but more vitally because we *need* to do so. No one keeps all of God's commandments. All have sinned [Romans 3:23], and we receive forgiveness of sins only through Jesus.)

The Authority of Scripture

The first of the Ten Commandments truly establishes the Lord God of the Bible, God in three persons, as the ultimate authority for our lives. Consequently this means that the Bible must be for us the absolute and final authority in all matters of which it speaks, for the Bible is the word and the will of the God revealed therein.

There can be no reservations in our surrender to the authority of the Bible. One cannot say, "I will obey it only up to a point," and still be fully submitted to the God whose Word it is. The point at which one begins to resist the authority of Scripture is the point at which he yields to another god.

You Must Choose

The first Commandment forces a decision upon every person. This inescapable decision is well put by Joshua: "Choose you this day whom ye will serve" (Joshua 24:15). What will be the ultimate authority in your life? Who will be supreme, who will reign as lord in your heart? May we prayerfully echo the words of Joshua: "As for me and my house, we will serve the Lord" (Joshua 24:15).

3

No Graven Images

*Basic Scripture resources: Exodus 20:4-6;
Deuteronomy 4:12-24; Acts 17:29;
Romans 1:18-24; Psalm 139:7-10; John 14:8-11*

"Thou shalt not make unto thee any graven image" (Exodus 20:4).

The second Commandment has an unusual history. In fact, some do not even consider it to be a separate commandment. Roman Catholics and Lutherans include it in the first Commandment. They see it merely as a continuation of the prohibition of idolatry. (In order to keep the list at *ten,* in accord with Deuteronomy 4:13, they then divide the tenth Commandment. "Thou shalt not covet thy neighbor's house" becomes the ninth; "thou shalt not covet thy neighbor's wife" becomes the tenth.)

Is it, then, intended to be a separate commandment, the second in a list of ten? Most likely it is. It deals not with idolatry as such, which is the worship of false gods. Rather, it deals with the making of *images* to represent the *true* God. The first Commandment establishes God alone as the only true God; He alone must be worshiped. The second Commandment speaks about the *manner* of worship: we must not try to worship Him through images intended to portray Him in any way.

Underlying this prohibition is one of the most basic truths or principles, namely, *the transcendent nature of our God.*

I. What Is Prohibited?

The second Commandment specifically prohibits the making of graven images in the form of created beings of any kind. Does this mean that a sculptor cannot make a statue of a bird, or that an artist cannot draw a picture of a cow? No, this is a prohibition not of images as such, but of images intended to represent the divine nature.

Again, this is not merely a prohibition of the worship of idols, such as Dagon the fish-god of the Philistines (see 1 Samuel 5). The worship of false gods is condemned by the first Commandment. The second Commandment forbids making and worshiping images of the true God. It attacks the very idea that God's holy and transcendent nature can be captured and represented in a physical form of any kind.

For instance, some Bible scholars think the golden calf made by Aaron (Exodus 32:4) was intended to be a visible representation of the Lord God. The same is thought of the two calves made by Jeroboam and placed in Dan and Bethel (1 Kings 12:28, 29). "Here is the God you worship," Aaron and Jeroboam were saying; "here is what He looks like."

"Stop it!" says God in the second Commandment. "No image you construct, no matter how beautiful and majestic, can be true to my nature. So do not even try it."

This commandment appears in other places. Deuteronomy 4:12-19 repeats it in a more specific way. The apostle Paul sums it up in Acts 17:29 thus: "Being then the offspring of God, we ought not to think that the Divine Nature is like gold or silver or stone, an image formed by the art and thought of man" (NAS). See Romans 1:21-23.

Someone may raise the question, *"Why* should such activity be prohibited?" The basic reason is that God's nature is uncreated, transcendent spirit. It is *impossi-*

ble to limit Him to a two-dimensional or three-dimensional form of *any* kind.

God is not like *any* created being. He is not like any thing "in heaven above," namely, He is not like a bird. Nor is He like any thing "in the earth beneath" (land animals) or "in the water under the earth" (fish). (See Exodus 20:4, and compare Deuteronomy 4:16-18.) He is not even like the physical form of human beings. (See Deuteronomy 4:16.)

A familiar fictional story has a first-grade teacher ask her pupils to draw a picture of just anything. Johnny gets a very serious look on his face and begins the task. The teacher passes his desk and inquires, "What are you drawing, Johnny?"

He replies, "A picture of God."

"But," says the teacher, "no one knows what God looks like."

"They will when I finish," he assures her solemnly.

Of course Johnny is mistaken in thinking that he knows what God looks like. But the teacher is also mistaken in assuming that God "looks like" something—we just don't know what. The fact is that God does not "look like" anything. He is not like any creature in our experience; His nature is beyond even our imagination.

Thus by forbidding attempts to make images of Him, God preserves His uniqueness as the only true God. He does not want to be associated with the pagan "nothings," whose only reality is in their representations!

Through this prohibition God helps us to maintain a high concept of His nature. Despite their good intentions, idol-worshipers tend to equate their gods with their idols. A purported statue of God would thus tend to limit God in our minds to one place. By prohibiting such images, God helps us remember that He is *not* limited by space, but is present everywhere at all times in a way that no statue or creature can be. (See Psalm 139:7-10.)

An image would only degrade God in our minds. Can a statue be greater than the one who carved it? Is not the living artisan more powerful than the lifeless stone or wood? How could we help losing confidence in a god made finite by a mortal's mind and hands? As someone has pointed out, there is something terribly demoralizing about seeing one's idols smashed.

Occasionally we see a work of art, such as Ernst Barlach's "Hovering God the Father," that attempts to depict the divine nature. This is the kind of sin prohibited by the second Commandment. Most of us, however, would not think of trying to draw a picture of God or carve a statue of Him. But sometimes we do form images of Him in our minds, such as the familiar elderly grandfather-type with flowing robe and beard. Though it may be difficult, we should try to guard against this tendency, for even this may cause us to limit our concept of the true God.

When we think of God, then, what kind of image should come to our minds? Why not Jesus? Christ our Lord is indeed the "real thing"; He is the perfect image of God.

Hebrews 1:3 says that Jesus "is the radiance of His glory and the exact representation of His nature" (NAS). "He is the image of the invisible God," says Colossians 1:15 (NAS). The apostle Philip once asked Jesus, "Lord, show us the Father, and it is enough for us." Jesus replied, "Have I been so long with you, and yet you have not come to know Me, Philip? He who has seen Me has seen the Father" (John 14:8, 9, NAS). Why, then, should we want any other image of God?

But, you may say, we do not know what Jesus really looked like. That is true, but it doesn't matter. It was not the *physical* nature of Jesus that resembled God anyway. It was His divine, *personal* nature. Since God

21

is personal, He can be represented to us only in a person, namely, Jesus. The kind of person Jesus was—loving, compassionate, forgiving, yet holy and just—is the character of our God.

If we know Jesus through the Gospel portraits, we do not *need* images of God. Jesus himself is that image.

This shows how important it is to study the Bible, especially the Gospel records of the life of Christ. What Jesus did, how He reacted to various situations, the attitudes He displayed, the kind of person He was, His character—all these are like windows into Heaven through which we get a glimpse of the divine nature, not with our physical eyes but with the eyes of our hearts (see Ephesians 1:18). Are we looking?

II. What Is Permitted

The second Commandment is sometimes misapplied and is taken to forbid certain things not actually included in its intended scope. For instance, ordinary art and photography are certainly not prohibited here. In the Bible God himself commanded certain images to be made for various purposes, such as the figures of the cherubim over the ark of the covenant (Exodus 25:18-20) and the serpent of brass (Numbers 21:8, 9).

Often the question arises whether pictures of Jesus can be permitted in light of this commandment. After all, Jesus is divine; He is God the Son, God incarnate. Since we are forbidden to make images of God, wouldn't it be wrong to depict Christ in art?

In reference to this question we must remember that Jesus was not only divine; He was also human. What is being portrayed in a picture of Christ is *not* His divine nature, but only His physical human nature. This is not wrong. It does not break the second Commandment. The divine nature of our Lord was not something visible to the eye; it cannot be captured on canvas.

Regarding pictures intended to represent Jesus, a few things should be remembered. First, in all probability we do not know what Jesus really looked like. Thus all portraits of Him are little more than guesses. Second, any picture of Christ should definitely be in good taste, with nothing that detracts from His holy and majestic character. Finally, images of Christ should not be used as vehicles of worship. They are best used in educational materials and as symbols of commitment.

Another serious misapplication of the second Commandment is the effort to find in it a mandate against the use of musical instruments in the worship of God. It should be obvious that those who use instruments in worshiping God are in no way equating them with God himself or thinking of them as representations of the divine nature!

This Commandment does, of course, presuppose that God is the Lord of worship and can dictate whatever form of worship He pleases. Whether instrumental music in worship pleases or displeases Him must be determined from other Scriptures. See Psalm 150:3-5; Revelation 5:8.

III. What Is Required

Pictures of Jesus on the wall or musical instruments in worship are neither prohibited nor required by the second Commandment. They are simply permitted; they are matters of opinion. A few things, mostly of a general nature, are required by this commandment, however. We will mention only two of them.

One thing required by this commandment is that we worship God according to *His* terms, not ours. Many things, of course, are left to our good judgment as informed by the general teaching of His Word. Other things are specifically mentioned as being essential to worship, whether it be individual or collective. For instance, we are taught to pray (Acts 2:42; 1 Timothy 2:1), to sing praises (Ephesians 5:19; 1 Corinthians 14:26), and to observe the Lord's Supper (1 Corinthians 11:23-26; Acts 2:42).

Another thing required by this commandment is that we seek God not through visible representations of His nature but rather through His revealed words. Compared with all false gods and idols, this is what is unique about the true God: He has *spoken!*

God mocks the idols of the nations thus:

> Their idols are silver and gold,
> The work of man's hands.
> They have mouths, but they cannot speak . . .
> They cannot make a sound with their throat.
> Those who make them will become like them,
> Everyone who trusts in them
> (Psalm 115:4-8, NAS).

Our God, however, is the *living God,* who speaks His will to our ears and hearts. This is the way we commune with Him: not by fawning over little statues, but by hearing and heeding His word.

The full force of this Commandment and of this particular point can be seen in Moses' comments to the people of Israel in Deuteronomy 4. He reminded them of their experience at Mount Sinai.

> Then the Lord spoke to you from the midst of the fire; you heard the sound of words, but you saw no form—only a voice. So He declared to you His covenant which He commanded you to perform, that is, the ten commandments; and He wrote them on two tablets of stone. . . . So watch yourselves carefully, since you did not see any form on the day the Lord spoke to you at Horeb from the midst of the fire; lest you act corruptly and

make a graven image for yourselves in the form of any figure, the likeness of male or female, the likeness of any animal that is on the earth, the likeness of any winged bird that flies in the sky, the likeness of anything that creeps on the ground, the likeness of any fish that is in the water below the earth. . . . So watch yourselves, lest you forget the covenant of the Lord your God, which He made with you, and make for yourselves a graven image in the form of any- thing against which the Lord your God has commanded you. For the Lord your God is a consuming fire, a jealous God (Deuteronomy 4:12, 13, 15-18, 23, 24, NAS).

"You did not see a form, but you did hear a voice." This is the point of the second Commandment. The Bible is God's voice speaking to us today. Let us hear it and heed it.

4

God's Holy Name

Basic Scripture resources: Exodus 20:7;
Matthew 5:33-37; 6:1-6; 7:21-23; 21:28-32;
Mark 7:5-8

The third Commandment states, "Thou shalt not take the name of the Lord thy God in vain." The basic principle embodied here is the majesty and holiness of the name of God. Because of its holy character, God's name must always be used with the utmost sincerity and reverence.

I. The Name of God

In our western culture there is a tendency to take an indifferent attitude toward names. "What's in a name?" we ask. Shakespeare has Juliet offer the familiar comment, "That which we call a rose, by any other name would smell as sweet" *(Romeo and Juliet,* II. 2).

Every parent has enjoyed choosing a name for his new offspring. What determines the choice? Occasionally a name is chosen because its meaning seems appropriate to the nature of the child or to the circumstances of his birth. But often it is simply a matter of aesthetic appeal: a certain name just sounds masculine, or daintily feminine, or cute. Often parents name their child after a friend or relative or after a Bible person.

In other words, we seldom make a direct connection between someone's name and his character.

The Importance of Names

This was not the case in Biblical times, when the concept of *name* was much more significant than now. In Bible days a person's name was meant to express his very essence or character. For instance, the name *Benjamin* means "son of my right hand," which exactly expressed the relationship between Jacob and his youngest son. The names *Joshua* and *Jesus* mean "salvation of the Lord," which succinctly sums up the mission and accomplishment of each.

The seriousness of one's name was shown particularly when the Lord changed the names of certain people. Their new names reflected more clearly their role and destiny in God's plan. For instance, God changed *Abram* (exalted father) to *Abraham* (father of a multitude) (Genesis 17:5).

This intimate relation between a person's name and the person himself made the use of the name a matter of great importance. A disrespectful use of a man's name indicated disrespect for the man himself.

God's Name and Nature

The Biblical attitude toward the name of God is no exception to the above. His name is holy and must be reverenced. "Holy and reverend is his name," says Psalm 111:9. Jesus began the model prayer with the words, "Our Father who art in heaven, Hallowed be thy name" (Matthew 6:9, ASV). Jesus was saying, "Let Your name be acknowledged as holy and treated reverently."

Why should this be? Because God's name stands for the very person of God himself. As G. D. Boardman says, the name of God "signifies his nature, his attributes, his character, his authority, his purposes, his methods, his providences, his words, his institutions, his truths, his kingdom; in short, all that God is, all that God says, all that God does, all that God bids" *(The*

27

Ten Commandments; Philadelphia: Judson Press, 1946 reprint, p. 85).

This intimate relation between God's name and nature is especially clear on several occasions. In Exodus 34:5-7, when the Lord graciously proclaims His name before Moses, this includes a proclamation of His basic nature and attributes. When a special divine messenger, an angel of the Lord, was sent to guide the Israelites through the wilderness, the Lord established his divine authority by announcing that "my name is in him" (Exodus 23:20, 21).

The Name of Jesus

The New Testament makes it clear that "the name of the Lord thy God" includes the name of each of the three persons of the triune God: God the Father, God the Son, and God the Holy Spirit. Jesus commanded His followers to baptize people "into the name [singular] of the Father and of the Son and of the Holy Spirit" (Matthew 28:19, ASV). The divine name embraces all three.

The significance and holiness of the name of Jesus is especially emphasized. The disciples performed miracles through the power of Jesus' name (Luke 10:17; Acts 3:16; 4:10; 16:18). Remission of sins, salvation, and eternal life are given through Jesus' name (Acts 10:43; John 20:31; Acts 4:12). We must believe on the name of Jesus (John 2:23; 3:18; 1 John 3:23) and be baptized in His name (Acts 2:38; 8:16; 10:48; 19:5).

The name of Jesus is the most exalted of all and demands the highest reverence and respect. Following Jesus' humiliation in death,

> God highly exalted him, and gave unto him the name which is above every name; that in the name of Jesus every knee should bow, . . . and

that every tongue should confess that Jesus Christ is Lord, to the glory of God the Father (Philippians 2:9-11, ASV).

The third Commandment applies with full force to the name of Jesus.

The Basic Meaning

In view of the importance of God's name, we see why we are commanded not to use it in vain. This means basically that we must not use it in a thoughtless, empty, irreverent, or hypocritical way.

II. Profanity

The most obvious application of this Commandment to Christian behavior is its prohibition of profanity or cursing, which is a kind of blasphemy.

To profane something means to take that which is uncommon, exalted, and holy, and to drag it down to the level of the common, ordinary, and impure. Thus we profane God's holy name when we use it simply as an expletive or swearword, to give vent to our anger, or to express strong feelings about something.

Profane Expressions

What kinds of expressions are prohibited as a profane use of God's name? The first to be mentioned (and they are listed here with reverence and trembling) are hard oaths such as "Good God!" or "By God!" or "My God!" or "God damn!" or simply "God!" To utter such expressions as deliberate profanity is the height of blasphemy.

But these are not the only expressions forbidden here. There are other somewhat "softer" oaths that are used even by the more pious but that are still a profaning of God's name. These include "I'll swear to God!" and "Great God Almighty!" and "Lord God!"

Even the expressions "Thank God!" and "God knows!" and "So help me God!" and "God bless America!" are vain and sinful if used in a careless, offhand way. Occasionally we hear someone lose his temper and begin to swear, "God—"; but then he catches himself and completes the oath with the words, "—bless America!" He thinks he has avoided the blasphemy, but his reckless disregard for the holiness of God's name has already manifested itself.

Since Jesus is our Lord and our God (John 20:28), and since His name is above every name (Philippians 2:9), then it is likewise blasphemous to use His name simply as a swearword. The person who carelessly says "For Christ's sake!" or "Jesus Christ!" is just as guilty as the one who says "God damn it!"

Many people, including many sincere Christians, profane the name of God by a thoughtless use of the word *Lord.* How often do we hear a sweet Christian lady carelessly say "Lord have mercy!" or "O Lord!" or just "Lord!" (Sometimes in the vernacular it becomes "Lordy!")

But is "Good Lord!" any less a profanity than "Good God"? He who is our God is our Lord also (see again John 20:28). When the average person hears the word *Lord,* of whom does he immediately think? Definitely not of an English nobleman, but rather of "the Lord our God." Hence we must use the word *Lord* with sincerity and reverence.

What about *damn* and *hell* when used simply as common swearwords? These too are profanity and are forbidden by this Commandment. Both expressions refer to something that is the exclusive prerogative of God, namely, eternal judgment; therefore any use of these terms brings God into the picture by implication. A light and flippant use of *damn* or *hell* is a mockery of God's judgment, and is thus a mockery of the power and person of God.

30

The Seriousness of Profanity

Profaning the name of God is a serious sin. The third Commandment specifies that "the Lord will not hold him guiltless that taketh his name in vain" (Exodus 20:7). Those who do so join the ranks of the enemies of God (Psalm 139:20).

The penalty prescribed by God for this sin shows its seriousness. Under the Old Testament law the punishment was death. Leviticus 24:10-23 gives the account of a young man who was overheard blaspheming the Lord's name. He was brought to Moses, and the Lord instructed Moses to have the man stoned to death: "And he that blasphemeth the name of the Lord, he shall surely be put to death, and all the congregation shall certainly stone him" (Leviticus 24:16).

There is an indication in the New Testament that Christians blasphemed were excommunicated from the church. In 1 Timothy 1:20 Paul refers to two men, Hymeneus and Alexander, "whom I have delivered unto Satan, that they may learn not to blaspheme." To "deliver unto Satan" means to excommunicate or to exclude from the fellowship of the church (1 Corinthians 5:5). It is the most serious penalty the church itself can inflict on its erring members.

Why is profanity or blasphemy such a serious sin? A person may be in the habit of using a term for God (e.g., *God, Christ,* or *Lord)* as a common expletive. "What's wrong with it?" he asks. "I don't mean anything by it." But that is just the point! The name of God is holy, and we are to use it only when we mean something by it. To use it in a meaningless or thoughtless way is an insult to God.

III. Hypocrisy

We may take God's name in vain in other ways besides thoughtless, blasphemous speech. We need not speak another person's name in order to use it. For instance, we may use another's name by taking it unto ourselves and wearing it or becoming associated with it in some way. A wife does this when she takes on the surname of her husband. This is also what a Christian does: he takes to himself the name of Christ his Lord.

When we are thus associated with a certain name, everything we do reflects upon it for good or for bad. In order to be true to that name, our whole life must be consistent with its reputation and character.

To use an example from the realm of fiction, the name *Walton* has become associated with all things pure and wholesome as a result of the television series about "The Waltons." But what if it were discovered that John-Boy Walton had become a dope peddler and a wino? Would that not disgrace the *name?*

Disgracing God's Name

The same kind of disgrace is caused when one who wears the name of God lives a carnal, worldly, selfish life. For instance, when Israel broke their covenant with God, their disobedience polluted His name, God said (Jeremiah 34:16).

Jesus roundly condemned the scribes and Pharisees for their hypocrisy. Through their public display of worship and careful observance of the ceremonial law, they gave the impression that they were true servants of God. But Jesus, calling them hypocrites, declared that their hearts were far from God (Mark 7:6). Their private lives were not at all consistent with their showy public profession (see Matthew 23:13-33).

In Romans 2:17-24 Paul declared that this kind of hypocrisy brought shame and disgrace to the name of God. "Thou that makest thy boast of the law, through breaking the law dishonorest thou God? For the name of God is blasphemed among the Gentiles through you" (Romans 2:23, 24).

Consequences of Hypocrisy

Wearing and using the name of Christ while living a sinful life has serious consequences. First it results in eternal damnation for the hypocrite himself, as Jesus says in Matthew 7:21-23.

Even more serious than this, however, is the fact that it results in the eternal damnation of many other souls. How many are turned away from Christ and His church by the hypocritical life of one who wears Christ's name? Any soul-winner will testify that the hypocritical church member is one of the greatest hindrances to evangelism and church growth.

Thus the third Commandment requires that we who wear the name of Christ live a life consistent with His holy name. We must be holy, as He is holy (1 Peter 1:16). "Let every one that nameth the name of Christ depart from iniquity" (2 Timothy 2:19).

5

Lord of Time

*Basic Scripture resources: Exodus 20:8-11;
Mark 2:23-28; Luke 4:16-22; 14:1-6;
Hebrews 10:25*

The basic principle that underlies the fourth Commandment is that God is the Lord of our time. He has the authority to tell us how to use it, and we must account to Him for each moment.

In this Commandment the Lord of time gives basic guidelines for the organization of our lives. He tells us how to use all seven days of each week. Six days must be devoted to work, while one day must be set apart as a day of special significance.

I. The Special Day

God instructed the Israelites to set apart the seventh day or Sabbath day as their special day. It was distinguished from the other days in that no work was to be done on it (Exodus 20:8-11; 31:14-17).

The Sabbath Rest

What was the purpose of this rest? Did God require it just because He knew that rest is essential for good health? No, the purpose was mainly religious.

The Sabbath rest was to honor God for redeeming Israel from Egyptian slavery. It called attention by contrast to the cruel labor from which God had saved them. It was a reminder that the nation owed its existence to God. Deuteronomy 5:15 says this:

Remember that thou wast a servant in the land of Egypt, and that the Lord thy God brought thee out thence through a mighty hand and by a stretched out arm: therefore the Lord thy God commanded thee to keep the sabbath day.

Why was the seventh day chosen? This was the day on which God rested from His work of creation. It was fitting that this be the Jews' day of rest. (See Exodus 20:11; 31:17).

From Sabbath to Lord's Day

Deliverance from Egyptian slavery was the high point in the religious heritage of Israel. It was fitting that their special holy day should commemorate that event. For Christians, however, the high point is something quite different and much more magnificent. It is our deliverance from the bondage of sin through the death and resurrection of Jesus! Thus it is proper that our special holy day should honor Jesus and His victory over sin.

With this change in the meaning of the special day has come a change in the day itself. The Jews kept the seventh day, but Christians observe the first day of the week (Sunday), which is called "the Lord's Day" (Revelation 1:10).

This raises an important question. Was this change of days authorized by God and introduced by the apostles? Some groups say it was not and that Christians must still keep the seventh day.

It is true that there is no direct New Testament command to observe the first day of the week. But other aspects of the Bible's teaching, as well as the apostolic practice, show that God has replaced the Sabbath with the Lord's Day.

The church came into existence on the first day, the day on which Pentecost fell (Acts 2). Under apostolic guidance local congregations continued to meet for worship on the first day, as Acts 20:7 and 1 Corinthians 16:2 show. Second-century Christian writers (Ignatius, Barnabas, and Justin Martyr) testify that Christians observed the first day of the week. (Early Christians such as Paul continued to visit Jewish synagogues on the Sabbath day to evangelize the already-gathered audiences. See Acts 13:5; 17:1-3; 19:8.)

According to the Old Testament, Sabbath observance was a sign between God and Israel (Exodus 31:13-17; Ezekiel 20:12), and therefore was not meant to last into the Christian age. Exodus 31:17 does say that it would last for ever, but here *for ever* means only "for as long as Israel exists as my special people." Similar language is used of other things that clearly are not parts of the Christian religion. Examples are the temple (1 Kings 9:3) and "perpetual" incense (Exodus 30:8).

The New Testament confirms this by clearly stating that Sabbath observance is no longer binding on anyone (Colossians 2:16).

The Day of Resurrection

The basic reason for observing the first day of the week is that this is the day on which Jesus arose from the dead. It is fitting to honor the Savior on the day when His victory was won.

The resurrection of our Lord was a monumental event comparable only to the original creation of the world. It was the beginning of a new creation, a new age. It is fitting that the mighty act that marked the beginning of the new creation should occur on the *first* day of the week.

Thus we no longer keep the seventh day, which signified the completion of the old creation. We celebrate the first day, the day of resurrection, the day of promise and hope for a new creation.

Lord's Day Observance

What is the proper way to observe the Lord's Day? Basically it should be used to honor and worship Christ the Redeemer. Attending public worship is an essential part of such observance. (See Acts 20:7; 1 Corinthians 16:2; Hebrews 10:25.)

Should the Lord's Day be a day of rest? Not necessarily. Contrary to popular belief, abstaining from work is not essential to Lord's Day observance. The Old Testament required rest on the Sabbath, but such resting does not have the religious significance for Christians that it did for Jews.

The most important point is that the Lord's Day must be kept special and holy; it must be set apart from the other days in a way that honors the Lord.

If one's work schedule requires him to work a shift on Sunday, he must take extra care to make the rest of the day special. He must be sure to attend one of the church's services. It is not failure to rest that violates the Lord's Day; it is failure to make it a special day for honoring Christ.

II. Labor Days

Though mainly concerned with the special day of the week, the fourth Commandment also says, "Six days shalt thou labor, and do all thy work" (Exodus 20:9). Herein the Lord establishes the moral responsibility for every human being to work.

The Necessity of Work

Why is everyone commanded to work? Many believe it was a part of the curse laid upon the human race as a result of Adam's sin. This is inferred from Genesis 3:17-19, in which God says to Adam, "Cursed is the ground for thy sake; in sorrow shalt thou eat of it all the days of thy life . . . in the sweat of thy face shalt thou eat bread."

This curse does involve man's working for a living, but this is not when God introduced the requirement for work. Even before man sinned, God commanded him to subdue the earth and have dominion over it (Genesis 1:28). Adam was put in the Garden of Eden to tend it (Genesis 2:15).

The curse in Genesis 3 affects not work's necessity but its circumstances. Work is no longer simply the creature's grateful and loving response to his Creator. Man must now work in order to live; he must sweat in order to eat. Thus there is pressure or burden upon man to work; it is a source of anxiety or sorrow.

If work is not a result of the curse, then what makes it necessary? It is necessary first of all because we are created in the image of God. God himself is active, not idle. Jesus said, "My Father worketh hitherto, and I work" (John 5:17). Because God works, those made in His image should also work.

Second, love for one another requires work. The non-worker must live as a parasite off the labor of others. But this is contrary to Christian love. The very nature of love is to give to others, not just to receive from them. Thus if we love one another, we must work to sustain ourselves and not selfishly take advantage of the labor of others.

Finally, work is necessary because man is a social creature. Subduing the earth is a cooperative enterprise, and each must carry his share of the load. Every day each one of us depends upon the labor of thousands of others. Such an interdependent society requires that all of us contribute to the vast pool of ideas, goods, and services from which everyone draws.

What Is Work?

This should lead us to a clearer understanding of the nature of work. Some tend to think of work only in

terms of manual labor. The word work c(
ideas of machines and muscles, sweat and

But this concept is too narrow. Basically w...
activity that helps to maintain and improve society. It
may be manual, but it may also be mental. A teacher
can work while reading a book. A writer can work
while staring out the window. If it adds to the general
welfare of mankind, it is work.

To see this should help us develop a better attitude
toward our daily occupations, which are neither a
curse nor just a means of making money. Seen only as
such, work often becomes boring drudgery, and the
workman loses pride and interest in his labor. The
result is shoddy products and indifferent service. But
when work is seen as contributing to the happiness of
others, it takes on new meaning. There is new incen-
tive to do work of higher quality, and there is more
personal satisfaction in a job well done.

The Sin of Sloth

The Bible condemns slothfulness, or the wilful neglect of work. (See Proverbs 6:6-11; 26:13-16.) Paul
says expressly, "If anyone will not work, neither let
him eat" (2 Thessalonians 3:10, NAS). To those not
working he says, "Now such persons we command
and exhort in the Lord Jesus Christ to work in quiet
fashion and eat their own bread" (2 Thessalonians
3:12, NAS).

Paul does not condemn those who *cannot* work, but
those who *will* not, those who deliberately refuse to
bear their share of the load. Such a manner of life
cannot be allowed because, as does any parasite, it
tends to destroy the very system that sustains it.

The Use of Leisure Time

How to use leisure time is a special problem today.
Automation, a larger labor force, a four-day work

week, longer vacations, and early retirement are giving workers more time away from their bread-winning occupations.

How will this leisure time be spent? The trend is toward using it for personal pleasure. Man-made lakes, large amusement parks, spectator sports, and television provide entertaining escapes from constructive activity. They are do-nothing retreats.

Herein lies the problem. Can we count this leisure time as our time, and squander it on pleasure-oriented, self-centered pastimes?

God commanded the Israelites to work six days each week. He thus intended for them to spend six-sevenths of their time subduing the earth and making a contribution to the development of society.

If we have more time away from our occupational work, we are not free to spend that time in just any way we please. We still have the obligation to work, that is, to do something constructive and useful for mankind. Many activities can contribute to the welfare of society in general. For instance, one can do volunteer church work or hospital work.

Some rest and relaxation, of course, are essential for a healthy mind and body. But we must be very careful not to let our increasing leisure time be dominated by self-centered recreation. God is the Lord of leisure time too.

6

Human Authority

Basic Scripture resources: Exodus 20:12;
Deuteronomy 6:6-9; Proverbs 23:22-25
Mark 7:9-13; Ephesians 6:1-4; 2 Timothy 1:5

Whereas the first Commandment enjoins submission to divine authority, the fifth Commandment requires submission to human authority. It establishes the principle of obedience in human relationships.

What is authority? Basically it is the power or right (1) to declare to others what shall be considered right and wrong, (2) to demand of others that they do what is right, and (3) to enforce right conduct by punishing evildoers. (See H. Hoeksema, *Love Thy Neighbor for God's Sake;* Grand Rapids: Eerdmans, 1955, p. 16.)

Obviously the only one who has such authority in an absolute sense is God. But God has chosen to set up certain spheres of authority within the human race. Within each of these He has appointed certain ones who exercise authority as His representatives.

There are at least three such spheres of authority. One is the state; another is the church. The third sphere is the family, with which the fifth Commandment specifically deals. Though the family is the smallest unit of authority, it is nevertheless the most important. Thus it is singled out for special attention.

I. The Family in God's Plan

The family is especially important because it plays the crucial role in establishing and maintaining proper authority in all spheres. It is primary and basic to all others, because it is in the home that one begins to learn obedience and submission.

To the growing child parental authority is representative or symbolic of all authority. The attitudes and patterns learned in the home determine how he will respond to authority in other spheres. When young people fail to learn how to honor father and mother, they will have little respect for teachers, policemen, and lawmakers. Rebellion in the home is a prelude to general lawlessness and social anarchy.

The Family Under Attack

The breakdown of the family is the result if not the explicit purpose of many trends and movements in our time. In light of its extreme importance in God's plan, it is no wonder that Satan is working so hard to destroy it. In doing so he uses many weapons, some old and some new.

Divorce continues to be one of Satan's major instruments of destruction. The "no-fault" divorce laws being enacted in some states make the dissolution of marriage a simple matter. Also, divorce is becoming more socially acceptable. Thus marriage and family solidarity are being taken less seriously.

Another factor working against the family is the covetousness of many parents. Sometimes a father will work long hours or hold two jobs just to provide unnecessary luxuries for his family. Often both mother and father work, making the children daytime orphans. True family life is sacrificed to mammon.

The current social revolution threatens the family from several directions. The "gay liberation" campaign is a movement away from the family as designed by God, and so are some elements of the "women's liberation" movement. The "new left" revolutionary movement seeks to turn youth against parents.

The Crisis in Authority

The result of these satanic assaults on the family is an increasing contempt for authority. Divine authority is mocked and scorned. There is open rebellion against the authority of the civil government; the law is defied and policemen derided as "pigs." In many public-school classrooms teachers are openly insulted and ignored. Parents are regarded as squares, and their values are considered to be outdated.

The erosion of the family unit is certainly a principal cause of this crisis. Youth not disciplined to submit to parental authority are presently asserting their freedom from all authority.

Honor for parents is thus not just tradition or sentiment or kindness. It is absolutely necessary for an orderly world. The family unit is the building block of society, the very foundation of the social order; and the fifth Commandment is the guardian of the family.

II. Respect for Parents

The fifth Commandment specifically requires children to honor their parents. This refers basically to an attitude of respect and reverence. Leviticus 19:3 even says, "Ye shall fear every man his mother, and his father." Here "fear" means godly reverence.

Submission in Youth

In childhood, honor for parents involves obedience, or submission to parental authority. Colossians 3:20 exhorts, "Children, obey your parents in all things: for this is well-pleasing unto the Lord." Ephesians 6:1, 2 puts it thus: "Children, obey your parents in the Lord: for this is right. Honor thy father and mother. . . ."

The crucial necessity for respect and obedience to parents cannot be overemphasized. In the Old Testament law God prescribed the severest penalties for dishonoring parents. Striking or even cursing a parent was punished by death (Exodus 21:15, 17). An incorrigibly rebellious son was likewise to be surrendered to the authorities and stoned to death by all the men of the city (Deuteronomy 21:18-21).

This severe procedure shows that disrespect for parents is not just a family matter; it is the concern of society as a whole. "All the men of his city" were to participate in the execution because the whole city was threatened by such a youth. If left unchecked, the attitude of rebellion grows and spreads to others; thus this evil must be removed from the community. The execution itself was to have a deterrent effect: "All Israel shall hear, and fear."

Care in Later Life

The command to honor father and mother applies to adults also. Though no longer required to obey parents, adults must show them honor in other ways.

Perhaps the best word to describe the attitude an adult should have toward his parents is *care.* We should care about our parents, and we should care for them if necessary.

Care means remembering: remembering via letters, calls, visits, and gifts. An elderly parent dreads few things more than being forgotten.

Jesus condemned the Pharisees who tried to escape their responsibility of providing for their parents by "donating" their possessions to the Lord (Mark 7:10-13). It was a "donation" only on paper; they continued to use everything as if it were their own.

III. Responsibilities of Parents

The fifth Commandment involves obligations for parents as well as for children. Respect for and submission to authority must be learned. It is not enough for a parent simply to give orders; a child must be taught how and why to obey.

Thus it is the parents' responsibility to nurture an obedient and respectful spirit in their children. If a child fails to learn respect for authority, his parents must share a large part of the blame.

Instruction in Righteousness

A parent's first and basic obligation to his children is to instruct them concerning God's works and God's law. Psalm 145:4 says, "One generation shall praise thy works to another, and shall declare thy mighty acts." Thus every parent must be a teacher.

In Old Testament times Hebrew parents were strictly commanded to teach their children the law of God, as Deuteronomy 6:6-9 emphasizes. Timothy's mother Eunice and grandmother Lois were faithful to this command (2 Timothy 1:5), and Timothy knew the Hebrew Scriptures (2 Timothy 3:15).

If this was required of Hebrew parents, do not Christian parents have an even greater duty to instruct their children in righteousness? Indeed, Paul commands fathers to rear their children "in the nurture and admonition of the Lord" (Ephesians 6:4).

Sunday school, church, and youth activities in the church should not be considered optional and left to the choice of the child. The same is true of Christian camps, retreats, and youth conferences, which are among the most effective teaching instruments today. Christian parents must see such programs as means of instructing their children in righteousness. Of course, they should use discretion in order to avoid provoking rebellion, and also take account of the special needs of shy or sensitive children.

Church programs, however, can never take the place of instruction in the home itself. Christian parents must constantly be teaching their children about Christ and Christian living. Every Christian home should have regular family devotions.

Occasionally a parent will say, "I'm not going to try to influence my children regarding religion. I want them to make up their own minds." Such an idea is irresponsible and un-Christian. If a parent loves his children, he will do everything in his power to influence them in the way of salvation.

Correction

The second basic responsibility of parents is correction. Instruction alone will not build respect for authority in the heart of a child; the teaching must be enforced with corrective discipline. (See Proverbs 13:24; 22:15; 23:13.)

Two extremes must be avoided. If a parent is too slack and inconsistent in discipline, this may lead to a contempt for authority. On the other hand, if the correction is too harsh and unjust, it may create anger and lead to rebellion. Thus Ephesians 6:4 warns, "And, ye fathers, provoke not your children to wrath."

In summary, the main point of the fifth Commandment is to establish the principle of authority and obedience in human relationships. Parental authority properly administered and duly respected is the chief means to the realization of this principle in all human relationships.

7

Respect for Human Life

Basic Scripture resources: Exodus 20:13;
Matthew 5:21-26; Mark 3:1-6; James 4:1, 2;
1 John 3:11-18

An anarchist shakes his fist in a policeman's face
and calls him an ugly name. A husband is so angry
with his unfaithful wife that he kills her. A man seethes
with hatred toward a person of a different race who
has just sat down beside him. A young girl enters a
"women's clinic" and has an abortion.

What do all these people have in common? They
have all shown contempt for human life. Thus they
have all broken the sixth Commandment; they are all
guilty of murder.

1. Human Life Is Sacred

The basic principle embodied in this command is
that *human life is sacred.* God has made man in His
own image. Therefore human life is more than just
animal life; it is a reflection of God's own life.

What Is Human Life?

Some people have a misguided reverence for life in
general, refusing to kill any animal or even insect. But
this ignores the sharp distinction between animal and
human life. Human life alone is made in the image of
God (Genesis 1:26, 27).

Man is unique because he is spirit as well as body.
Thus human life is more than physical; it includes a

spiritual dimension as well. Human life in its fullness is the life of the whole person, his spirit and his body.

Thus this commandment involves not just the killing of someone's body, but also the destruction or damaging of his spirit or character or personality.

Life and Love

The basic requirement of this command is a right attitude toward human life and personality. The Bible clearly teaches that the attitudes of the inner man are primary and are the roots from which all outward actions stem. Murder is in a man's heart before it is on his hands (Matthew 15:18, 19).

The right attitude toward all human life is summed up in the word *love*. Loving our neighbor means having a loving respect and concern for his life. We will do nothing to violate his life or personality. We will do everything we can to preserve and enhance his life.

II. What Is Forbidden?

Clearly there are many ways to violate human life. We may kill in thought and word as well as in deed.

Murder in Thought

Many different attitudes and thoughts of the heart are nothing less than murder. One such attitude is hatred. "Whosoever hateth his brother is a murderer," says 1 John 3:15. Hatred is a feeling of strong dislike and aversion, a feeling of loathing and abhorrence, a desire to inflict evil upon someone or destroy him.

Someone may object, "I can't help the way I feel." But hatred is more than feeling. It is rooted in the intellect and is an act of the will. Only when the intellect judges someone to be objectionable and evil does the will develop an attitude of hatred toward him.

Malicious, prolonged anger toward a fellow human being is also murder (Matthew 5:21, 22; James 1:19).

This deadly sin is born from selfish motives: personal jealousy, wounded pride, or a desire for revenge. It can be avoided if our heart is God-centered instead of self-centered.

Holding a grudge, refusing to forgive, and desiring to "get even" are murderous attitudes. Indeed, any ill will toward another, including a desire to injure him or to see him injured, is thought-murder.

Murder in Word

Murderous thoughts often escape our hearts through our tongues. Hateful anger leads to scornful insults. Jesus names two such insults in Matthew 5:22. One is "Raca," which means "empty-head" and is comparable to such insults as "You dummy! You ignoramus! You stupid jerk!" The other is "You fool!"

Malicious ridicule or derision also damages the spirit. This includes scornful names for ethnic groups, as well as contemptuous mocking of someone's handicap or weakness or misfortune.

Word-murder is most clearly seen in threats and curses. Saying to another "Damn you!" or "Go to hell!" demonstrates the ultimate disrespect for him. To wish someone physically dead is bad. But to wish him to spend eternity in the place of punishment prepared for the devil is the epitome of hatred.

Murder in Deed

Indifferent disregard for the sacredness of human life may lead to overt acts of murder. Such acts may involve actual killing, or they may be destructive while stopping short of the actual taking of life.

The most obvious form of murder is homicide. This is the deliberate, unlawful killing of another person. Jesus says it is satanic (John 8:44).

Not all killing is murder. The Bible clearly distinguishes between accidental killing and deliberate killing (Exodus 21:12, 13; Numbers 35:9-34). A distinction is also made between unlawful killing and judicial killing. The law of Moses prescribed capital punishment for several crimes, including homicide (Exodus 21:12-16; 22:18-20).

Another form of murder is suicide. It may be commendable to lay down one's life for others (John 15:13), but suicide is definitely sinful, for it is motivated not by love but by enmity against God and hatred of one's position and circumstances.

In recent years a debate has been raging concerning abortion, which is the voluntary killing of a living baby growing within its mother's womb. In 1973 the United States Supreme Court declared all state laws prohibiting abortion to be unconstitutional. It spelled out a few guidelines that must be followed for abortions performed in the later stages of pregnancy, but in effect it made it legal for anyone to have an abortion who wants one. The Court's decision was based on the premise that the growing baby is not a person in the full sense of the word until it is actually born or can live outside the womb; hence it is not protected by the constitutional "right to life" until that time.

Only two points can be made briefly here. First, from a scientific and medical point of view, from the moment of conception the developing embryo possesses in latent form all the characteristics of a complete human being. Second, from the Biblical standpoint, an individual is considered to be a person while still in the mother's womb. See Psalm 139:13-15; Jeremiah 1:5; and Luke 1:39-44.

There really is no ground for denying the personhood of the developing embryo or baby in the womb. The baby is a person in the fullest sense of the word; to kill it is a violation of the sixth Commandment. Abortion is murder. Its only possible justification would be in the case where a choice must be made between the life of the mother and the life of the baby. In such a case it would be the lesser of two evils, but would still be an evil. Fortunately, because of the advances of modern medical technology, this choice is becoming more and more infrequent.

Some actions violate the sixth Commandment even if they do not result in the death of the person assaulted. For instance, any kind of physical violence inflicted with the malicious desire to injure someone is done in the spirit of murder.

The same is true of careless and irresponsible acts that lead to injury or death. Reckless driving is such an action; and if it results in death, the driver is charged with homicide by vehicle.

Actions that harm one's own body and are a threat to health and life are prohibited too. "Thou shalt not kill" by overwork, overweight, or smoking.

III. Problem Decisions

A word must be said about two problems that involve killing, namely, capital punishment and war.

Many oppose capital punishment, and the tide of judicial decision seems to be turning against it. Many Christians also feel that it is wrong, and often the sixth Commandment is quoted as prohibiting it.

Such a conclusion, however, is contrary to the entire teaching of Scripture. We have already noted that not all killing is murder, and that the Old Testament even prescribes death for certain crimes. This shows that capital punishment is not inherently wrong or contrary to the will of God.

But what about the New Testament age? Has Jesus given us a way of love and non-resistance that rules out capital punishment? No. In Matthew 5:38-48 He forbids personal vengeance, as does Paul in Romans 12:17-21. But in the latter context the inspired apostle clearly shows that God executes His own vengeance on evil-doers through the civil government (Romans 13:1-4). In comparing Romans 12:19 with Romans 13:4, we see that even in the Christian era capital punishment is God's own vengeance on the evildoer.

Participation in warfare must be considered on the same basis as capital punishment. It is the God-given duty of the civil government to maintain an environment where justice and righteousness prevail and where we can live our Christian lives unhindered (Romans 13:3, 4; 1 Timothy 2:1, 2; 1 Peter 2:13, 14). This must be done even if the government has to resort to the sword. A soldier who participates in warfare on behalf of his government (not in a spirit of personal revenge) is not breaking the sixth Commandment.

War may be murderous, of course, if a nation launches an unjustified attack on an unoffending neighbor just to gain more wealth or power or territory for itself. In some cases honest men may have different opinions about whether a certain war is justified or not, but we cannot say the Bible forbids wars in all cases.

Conclusion

When we consider the many implications of the sixth Commandment, we are overwhelmed at the breadth of its application. It shows that we cannot pass lightly over the laws of God, and it shows how very few of our choices and actions escape the scrutiny of His Word.

8

Marriage and Sex

Basic Scripture resources: Exodus 20:14;
Matthew 5:27-32; John 8:3-11; Romans 1:24-32;
1 Corinthians 6:13b-20; Ephesians 5:21-33.

In the seventh Commandment God establishes the principle of *the sanctity of the marriage relationship.* In the original purity of the Garden of Eden God ordained and blessed marriage and everything related to it (see Genesis 2:18-24). The expression "holy matrimony" is thus appropriate.

Since marriage is good and holy, it must be respected, honored, and protected. Anything that perverts, threatens, or destroys the marriage relationship is forbidden by God. This is why the seventh Commandment specifically condemns adultery.

This chapter will discuss the nature of marriage, its relation to sex, and the sins that violate it.

I. The Nature of Marriage

Marriage is not just a social convenience that has developed through some mythical process of evolution. It was deliberately designed by God as part of the original creation. Hence to understand the nature of marriage, we must turn not to the sociologist or the marriage counselor, but to the Word of God.

A Complementary Relationship

The Bible tells us first of all that marriage is a complementary relationship. Neither man nor woman was made to live a solitary life. Each without the other is incomplete. But when joined together, each complements or completes the life of the other.

Read Genesis 2:18-25. After the creation of Adam, God said, "It is not good that the man should be alone; I will make him a help meet for him." The "help meet for him" means a helper that corresponds to him or is suitable for him.

Before creating the woman, God required Adam to survey the entire animal kingdom. In this way Adam was made acutely aware that he was *alone.* Despite the abundance of other living creatures, he found none that corresponded to him (verses 19, 20).

Then God made the woman from the rib of the sleeping man. When Adam awoke and saw her, he immediately identified with her: "This is now bone of my bones, and flesh of my flesh" (verses 21-23).

The inspired writer then adds a divine commentary on this episode: "Therefore shall a man leave his father and his mother, and shall cleave unto his wife: and they shall be one flesh" (verse 24). Thus man and woman were literally "made for each other." They are intended to complement each other in marriage. They do not stand separately as two independent and self-sufficient individuals. Together they form one whole, one flesh.

"One flesh" here certainly refers to sexual union, but it also includes much more. Man and wife actually become one *life* as they share with one another their feelings, aspirations, desires, fears, weaknesses, strengths, possessions—indeed, their very selves.

It is a fact, of course, that many people do not marry, whether by choice or otherwise. Some even glorify singleness, as if it were a higher, more spiritual state than being married. Certainly marriage is not commanded; one does not *have* to be married in order to be pleasing to God. Also, it is true that it may be better in some circumstances to remain single, as Paul explains in 1 Corinthians 7.

Nevertheless the fact remains that God designed men and women to marry, and only in this state are their lives complete.

An Exclusive Relationship

It is also clear from the Word of God that marriage is an exclusive relationship. The two who become one flesh form a complete unit. The old saying, "Three's a crowd," definitely applies in this case. There can never be a third party involved in a true marriage.

In Old Testament times God permitted certain practices, such as concubinage and divorce, that infringed upon the intended exclusiveness of marriage. Commenting only on divorce, Jesus said that God allowed such a thing at that time because of the hardness of the people's hearts. He stressed that "from the beginning it was not so" (Matthew 19:8).

The marriage relationship is necessarily exclusive because it is patterned after the solitary devotion of the one God to His people. (See 2 Corinthians 11:2; Ephesians 5:22-33.) God is faithful to His people, and He demands that His people be faithful to Him. We can no more divide our love and loyalty between two spouses than we can between two gods.

A Loving Relationship

Finally, marriage is a loving relationship. A husband and wife must feel themselves bound together not just by law or necessity, but by love.

This aspect of the marriage relationship is also based upon God's nuptial relation to His people. (See Isaiah 62:4, 5; Hosea 2:19; 11:4.) Christ's love for His bride, the church, is specifically given as the pattern and example for husbands to follow (Ephesians 5:25-33).

When Paul exhorts husbands to love their wives (Ephesians 5:25), he is not referring to romantic sexual love. He is speaking here of the uniquely Christian love, *agape. Agape* is genuine, unselfish, self-giving concern for the happiness and welfare of the other person. This is the kind of love Christ showed for the church when He gave himself for it. Husbands and wives who share this kind of love experience marriage as God meant it to be.

II. Sex and Marriage

God has created us as sexual beings, male and female (Genesis 1:27). Sex is as much a part of our nature as is eating and laughing and working. This does not mean, however, that it must not be kept under control. God himself has told us how it must be regulated.

Specifically, the sexual relationship was designed by God to be a part of marriage. The sexual aspect of marriage is intended to reinforce the love and oneness that are the very essence of marriage. (See again Genesis 2:18-24.) Thus sexual union involves much more than physical contact; indeed, it should be an expression of the ultimate spiritual commitment that each partner has made to the other.

Sex was made for marriage, and not marriage for sex. Paul does advise a person to marry if his sexual drive makes fornication an unbearable temptation (1 Corinthians 7:1-9.) But this does not make marriage simply legalized sexual opportunity. Such an idea degrades both marriage and sex. It makes marriage basically a self-gratifying rather than a self-giving relationship, and it makes sex a selfish act even within marriage.

Sex is not shameful and impure, as some people think. Rather, the Bible pictures it as a profound, wholesome, honorable, enjoyable expression of married love. This is the role implied for it in Genesis 2:18-25. Hebrews 13:4 expressly says that "marriage is honorable in all, and the bed undefiled." With an earthy tenderness and a holy sensuality, the Song of Solomon celebrates the intimate delights of nuptial sex.

Since sexual union serves to strengthen the bonds of marital companionship and love, it is still quite legitimate and desirable even when procreation is not in view. Hence the wise use of contraceptives is compatible with God's intention for married sex.

III. Sex and Sin

Because of the profound relation between sex and marriage, it is evident that sexual relations outside the bond of holy matrimony are contrary to the will and purpose of God. Thus the Bible specifies and condemns a number of sexual sins.

Sinful Practices

"Thou shalt not commit adultery" is the prohibition of the seventh Commandment. Adultery is the sexual involvement of a married person with anyone other than his spouse. Such activity violates the oneness of the husband-wife relationship and tends to destroy the marriage bond itself. The New Testament continues to condemn it (1 Corinthians 6:9, 10; Hebrews 13:4), and it is the only legitimate ground for divorce that Jesus mentions (Matthew 19:9).

The Bible also condemns fornication. This term is used in two ways. Sometimes it means immorality in general, or simply unlawful sexual intercourse. This is obviously its meaning in Matthew 19:9, where it is used in the sense of adultery. More often, though, it has the specific meaning of the sexual involvement of an unmarried person. This sin, commonly called "premarital intercourse," is forbidden in 1 Corinthians 6:9, 10, 13-20; Galatians 5:19-21; Ephesians 5:3.

Another sexual practice that is condemned is homosexualism (Romans 1:24-27; 1 Corinthians 6:9, 10). Under the law of Moses, those practicing homosexualism were to be put to death (Leviticus 20:13).

A distinction is usually made between homosexuality, which is the unsought possession of homosexual tendencies, and homosexualism, which is the willful involvement in homosexual acts. The former is treated as a disease to be cured; the latter is condemned as sin.

A person who has homosexual tendencies (i.e., a homosexual or a lesbian) need not indulge in homosexual acts. Indeed, he cannot do so and still be obedient to God's law. Like the alcoholic, he must learn to control his appetite until the grace of God delivers him from his unnatural desires.

On the other hand, many people who are not homosexuals as such do engage in homosexual acts and seek homosexual contacts just for the sake of perverted pleasures and thrills. Such casual, unprovoked behavior may be even more wicked than homosexual activity by one who has an actual tendency in this direction.

Such practices as these are and always will be sins, because of the very nature of man and woman, and because of the very nature of marriage. The current widespread attempts to excuse such acts under the guise of a "new morality" are contrary to the will of God.

Sinful Lusts

Sexual sins can be committed in the heart alone. One such sin is lust, which is the mere desire for unlawful sexual relations. Jesus says that one who lusts after another has already committed adultery in his heart (Matthew 5:27, 28).

The Bible condemns lasciviousness, which is a kind of habitual lust, a constant dwelling on lustful thoughts (Galatians 5:19; Ephesians 4:19).

If lust is wrong, then so is anything that stimulates lust in oneself or in others. This is why the following things are wrong: certain kinds of dancing, immodest dress (1 Timothy 2:9), petting, suggestive flirting, and "dirty" literature and movies.

Sin and Forgiveness

Like all other sins, sexual sins make us guilty before God and incur His wrath. But like all other sins, they can be forgiven. Just as Jesus forgave the woman taken in adultery in John 8:3-11, so does God forgive all such sins for which we truly repent. So must we be willing to forgive others who have committed such sins. Adultery need not necessarily result in divorce; true repentance on the part of the adulterer or adulteress should elicit forgiveness from the wronged mate.

Better than the prayer for forgiveness, however, is the prayer that God will help us to avoid these sins in the first place.

9

Steal No More

Basic Scripture resources: Exodus 20:15;
1 Kings 21:1-19; Amos 8:4-7; Mark 12:41-44;
Luke 19:1-10; Ephesians 4:28; James 2:14-17.

The concept of private property is ancient and universal. Even a small child understands the meaning of "*my* toy" or "*my* doll." Most of us simply presuppose this right and have developed general patterns of living in accord with it.

The right to own private property should not be taken for granted, however. The Christian should realize that it is a privilege granted by God and guarded by His Word. The eighth Commandment, "Thou shalt not steal," specifically establishes the principle of *the sanctity of private ownership.*

The private ownership of property and goods is a right that must be recognized and respected by all. It involves more than rights, however. It also involves responsibilities that an owner must be willing to bear. This chapter will attempt to set forth both rights and responsibilities.

I. Private Property

The ultimate and primary owner of all things is God. He owns everything because He created it all. Psalm 24:1, 2 says, "The earth is the Lord's, and the fulness thereof; the world, and they that dwell therein. For he hath founded it upon the seas, and established it upon the floods." (See Psalm 50:7-12; Haggai 2:8.)

Although God is the primary owner of all things by right of creation, He has granted to us the rights and responsibilities of secondary ownership. He did this in the very beginning when He created man and woman and directed them to subdue the earth and have dominion over everything in it (Genesis 1:26-28).

This mandate to *subdue* the earth shows that private ownership is not achieved apart from work. It shows that God expected man to acquire private property by means of *personal labor.* This same point is seen in Ephesians 4:28, which says, "Let him that stole steal no more: but rather let him labor, working with his hands the thing which is good." Theft is the unlawful acquiring of property, but labor is the God-intended means for earning it.

Marxist communism as an economic system denies this Biblical teaching. A basic communistic doctrine is that all the means of producing goods, including raw materials and machinery and factories, belong to the state. Private enterprise is thus totally abolished. The only private property allowed under communism consists of goods for personal consumption.

Apart from the full reality of private ownership, however, the eighth Commandment is meaningless. The very fact that God has prohibited stealing means that He has placed His stamp of approval on the individual's right to own property. This command both presupposes and protects this right, and it forbids any encroachment upon it.

II. Stealing

The sanctity of private ownership demands that each person respect the right of others to own property. Thus the law of God (not just of the state) prohibits stealing, which is anything that violates this right of private ownership, or anything that deprives another of his own property.

Secret Theft

There are many ways to steal. One of the most common is ordinary theft. This involves taking someone else's property in a secret, stealthy manner, by which one hopes to avoid notice.

The scene that most of us call to mind when such theft is mentioned is that of a burglar as he pries open a window in the rear of a house or store and then proceeds to cart away the silverware or loot the cash register. Few people steal in this manner, however. The most common forms of theft are much less open and spectacular, yet they are theft just the same.

One such way of stealing is shoplifting, which is becoming more and more common. Many try to justify it by stealing from large stores and saying, "They are so big they will never miss it." They do miss it, of course; and in the end the ones who suffer are the store's customers, who are charged higher prices in order to make up for the loss. What we must realize is that stealing is stealing, whether it be from a pauper or from a millionaire. The greatest harm is not to the victim's purse but to the thief's heart.

"Employee theft" or "white collar theft" is another very widespread practice. Many millions of dollars' worth of goods and equipment disappear from offices, stores, and factories each year. They are pilfered by trusted employees, many of whom feel they are doing nothing wrong. But again, such actions are theft. A Christian will respect his employer's property, whether it be a power saw or a paper clip.

A slightly different kind of theft is plagiarism. This occurs when one writer deliberately quotes from another without giving credit, pretending that the stolen ideas are his own. Thefts of this kind occur on all levels, from students preparing term papers, to executives writing reports, to writers submitting manuscripts to publishers.

Robbery by Force

Another form of stealing is robbery by force, a situation in which the robber forces a person to turn over his money or possessions simply by overpowering him or by threatening him with harm.

This includes anything from ordinary robbery of the "stick-em-up" type to the illegitimate confiscation or nationalization of private property by a strong-armed government. It also includes kidnaping and looting, as well as the more "genteel" crimes of bribery and extortion.

An even more subtle form of robbery by force is the unjust labor strike, in which a single-minded group of people openly extorts money and other concessions from an employer under threat of harm. The employer himself is threatened with economic harm as a result of the shut-down of his business. Fellow-workers are threatened with physical harm if they attempt to continue working. The public is harmed by being deprived of necessary goods and services, and by being forced to bear the burden of higher labor costs.

Such robbery by force, in any of its forms, arises from a basic contempt for the property rights of others. It stands condemned by the eighth Commandment.

Robbery by Deceit

Another form of theft that is very widespread is robbery by deceit. The technical name for this is fraud. It occurs frequently in the area of business and trade. A merchant can rob a customer by falsely labeling his goods with regard to weight, count, and quality. A customer can rob a merchant by deliberately incurring an unpayable debt and declaring bankruptcy. The Bible condemns such fraudulent practices in Amos 8:4-7.

Other common forms of fraud include entering false information on one's tax form or falsifying an insurance claim. Housewives and merchants often conspire to defraud manufacturers by cashing "cents-off" promotional coupons when the specified products have not been bought. Most coupons clearly state that such a practice is fraud.

In the eyes of many people this kind of robbery is a very mild sin, if indeed it is considered sin at all. Thus even Christians are often guilty of it without fully realizing the seriousness of their deeds. In principle, however, it is no different from any other theft. Even though many people are doing it, and seem to be getting away with it, it is still wrong. The eighth Commandment forbids it.

Steal No More!

All forms of stealing are rooted in a kind of covetousness, namely, an unlawful desire to possess that which belongs to someone else. The evil consequences of such desire are clearly seen in the account of Naboth's vineyard (1 Kings 21:1-19).

To avoid the temptation to steal, we must learn to conquer covetousness. We must learn to respect the sanctity of private ownership. We must also learn that life does not consist in the abundance of the things we possess (Luke 12:15).

Like any sin, stealing can be forgiven if one truly repents and turns to God. True repentance demands that restitution be made wherever possible, though.

III. Stewardship

The concept of private property requires us not only to respect the property rights of others, but also to be conscientious stewards of our own possessions. We must remember that what we call "our own personal property" ultimately belongs to God; we are only stewards of it. We are required to use it for God's glory, and we must give account of it to Him.

Good stewardship requires us to be frugal and thrifty in our use of natural resources and products derived therefrom. Affluence is no excuse for wastefulness. No matter how much money a person has, he has no right to discard anything before its usefulness has been exhausted. Along this same line, public officials are obligated to be thrifty with regard to public funds and public natural resources.

Good stewardship also requires us to give a proportionate amount of our income to the work of God's church. Failure to do so is specifically called robbery by God's prophet (Malachi 3:8-10). In God's sight the *amount* one gives has never been as important as the proportion or *percentage* of one's income that one gives. Proportionate giving is the only system that God has ever authorized, even in the New Testament (1 Corinthians 16:2). Jesus praised the poor woman who gave a large percentage of her possessions (Mark 12:41-44).

Good stewardship finally requires sharing with those who are in need. See Ephesians 4:28; James 2:14-17; Acts 2:44, 45; 4:34-37.

Private property is a means of power, either for good or for evil, depending on one's attitude toward it and the use of it. One can use it to enrich himself at the expense of others, or one can use it to help others to the glory of God. The latter is good stewardship.

10

Truth Is Basic

*Basic Scripture resources: Exodus 20:16;
23:1-3; Proverbs 19:9; Acts 5:1-11;
Ephesians 4:25-32; James 1:26; 3:1-12*

The ninth Commandment says, "Thou shalt not bear false witness against thy neighbor" (Exodus 20:16). This clear law against lying is grounded upon one of the most basic principles of all: the sanctity of truth.

In this age of relativism, people are not as concerned about truth as they once were. There was a time when someone like Pilate could ask, "What is truth?" (John 18:38), and everyone assumed that the question could be answered. Today the question is different. People are asking, "Is anything true?" and the common answer is no.

With this rejection of any absolute and ultimate truth has come an increasing indifference toward truth in general. For many, honesty is no longer the best policy. Telling the truth is not as important as it used to be.

Thus we cannot be reminded too often of the reality of truth and the necessity of truth-telling. The purpose of this chapter is to give such a reminder.

I. The Necessity of Truth

Why is lying wrong? Why is telling the truth necessary? Is there any good reason why God should require us to be truthful? Is it purely an arbitrary requirement?

The answer, of course, is that truth and truth-telling are not at all arbitrary but are quite essential to our authentic existence as human beings. Truth and truthfulness are the very core of right relationships to God and to our fellow men. Lying and falsehood are contrary to the very nature of things.

God and His Image

It is God's own eternal and unchanging nature to be true. As Paul says, even if every human being is found to be a liar, God will still be true (Romans 3:4). Jesus is called "the truth" (John 14:6), and the Holy Spirit is called "the Spirit of truth" (John 16:13). When God speaks, His word is truth (John 17:17).

On the other hand, it is Satan who is the father of lies and liars. Jesus said, "When he speaketh a lie, he speaketh of his own: for he is a liar, and the father of it" (John 8:44).

Since we are made in the image of God, truth and truth-telling are proper to our nature. When we lie and deceive, we pervert our own God-given nature and prostitute ourselves to Satan. If we are going to be conformed to the image of the one who created us, we must stop all lying and be truthful (Colossians 3:9, 10). Just as lying and deceit are contrary to the nature of God, so are they contrary to true human nature.

Truth and Society

Truth is necessary not only as an ingredient in genuine human existence, but also as the very foundation of a decent society. Loving and meaningful relationships with our fellow men are impossible unless we assume that truth-telling is the normal and expected behavior.

This point is taught to us in Ephesians 4:25, which says, "Wherefore putting away lying, speak every man truth with his neighbor: for we are members one of another." The reason we should be truthful is that we are members one of another. We are interdependent members of one society: what affects one affects all. A lie that hurts one hurts all. The more prevalent lying becomes, the less any one of us will be trusted. Unless truth is the norm, society gives way to the law of the jungle: every man for himself.

II. Lie Not One to Another!

Because truth is so essential, the ninth Commandment and the Bible in general forbid all lying. "Lie not one to another," says Colossians 3:9.

What is a lie? It is the deliberate misrepresentation of what one judges in his mind to be the truth. An honest mistake is not a lie. On the other hand, one may say something that is true, and yet be guilty of lying—if he actually thinks the opposite is true and he deliberately intends to misrepresent it. In other words, whether a statement is a lie or not depends on the intention of the speaker.

For instance, suppose one Sunday morning Joe asks his dad if he can go with his friend to the latter's church. He gets permission; but instead of going to church, he and his friend sneak off and play ball.

When the family arrives at church, the minister asks Joe's mother if he will be in Sunday school. "Oh, yes," she says. "He went to church with his friend." Of course, the statement is not true, but she thinks it is. Thus she is not lying; she is merely mistaken.

But when the Sunday-school teacher asks Joe's little sister if he will be in church, the story is different. Sister just happens to be unhappy with Joe about something, so she tries to make him look bad. "No," she says, "he skipped church today and is out playing ball!" Even though what she says is true, she has lied, because in her mind she thinks Joe is in church. She is deliberately misrepresenting what she thinks is the truth.

False Witness

The kind of lying most specifically forbidden by the ninth Commandment is exactly what Joe's sister is guilty of, namely, speaking falsely against another person.

The law of Moses expressly condemns false accusations and false testimony in a court of law. "Thou shalt not raise a false report," says Exodus 23:1. The seriousness of this sin in God's sight is seen in Deuteronomy 19:16-21, where the following rule is laid down. If a man gives false testimony against someone in court, then whatever penalty would have been given to the innocent party because of the lie shall be applied to the liar instead.

Bearing false witness is wrong whether it occurs inside or outside a courtroom. James 4:11 gives the general prohibition, "Speak not evil one of another, brethren." All slander, libel, and false gossip are forbidden.

Falsehood and Deceit

False witness against another person is only one kind of lying. There are many other ways to lie, and all of them are wrong. Any attempt to deceive another person, whether it be by word or by action, whether it be by what is said or by what is left unsaid, is lying.

Temptations to lie face us every day. We are tempted to make false excuses in order to avoid a disagreeable chore or engagement: "I can't come to the meeting; I have a terrible headache." We are tempted to make false promises just to get rid of a pest: "Yes, Junior, I'll buy you a pony. Now let me finish my paper." We are tempted to withhold information and thus leave the wrong impression: (to a ticket-taker) "Sally's eleventh birthday was June 23; so she doesn't need a ticket." (Of course, it was June 23 two years ago, but nobody asked about that!) We are tempted to exaggerate: "This is a very economical car; it gets around twenty miles per gallon." (That is, on long slow trips it gets thirteen, but that's somewhere around twenty, isn't it?)

Certain professions offer greater temptations to deceive than others. In the business field, we must realize that false advertising and false claims about products for sale are just plain lying and thus are forbidden. Politicians must guard against false promises. Newsmen must realize that false or misleading news reporting is nothing less than lying.

Cheating in school is also lying, since the cheater deliberately misrepresents someone else's work as his own.

Hypocrisy is also a form of lying. A person may live a lie, pretending to be someone he is not, even though no words are actually spoken.

God wants us to see just how wicked all these forms of lying are. Thus He attaches the severest condemnation to them. "A false witness shall not be unpunished, and he that speaketh lies shall perish" (Proverbs 19:9). "All liars" shall be cast into the lake of fire, which is the second death (Revelation 21:8).

III. Speak the Truth in Love

On the positive side, the ninth Commandment requires us, in the words of Ephesians 4:15, to speak "the truth in love."

Truth in and of itself is basic, and we must always try to be truthful. But as everyone knows, the truth at times can hurt. Thus the Word of God exhorts us to speak the truth, but to do it in love. This means that we have a Christian duty to be tactful. Tact is not truth modified by falsehood, but truth softened by kindness.

Many people are proud of themselves for always "telling it like it is," for "not pulling any punches," for "laying it all on the line and letting the chips fall where they may." But malicious bluntness is a sign of weakness, not strength. It shows a lack of love and consideration for the feelings of others. We must speak the truth, but in love.

The love requirement rules out certain forms of communication, even though what is said may be true. This is why gossip is forbidden, even if it is true gossip. (This is a kind of backbiting.) Some other forms of truth that show a lack of love are revealing the secrets of others, bragging, and flattering people in order to influence them.

Finally, speaking the truth in love requires us to bear witness to our unsaved neighbors concerning their lostness and concerning the free gift of salvation offered to them through Jesus Christ. By remaining silent we leave the impression that everything is all right with them, when we know in our hearts that it is not. The greatest truth that we can speak to them is that Jesus saves, and love requires us to speak it!

11

The Peril of Greed

*Basic Scripture resources: Exodus 20:17;
Ecclesiastes 5:10—6:2; Matthew 20:20-28;
Luke 12:13-21; 1 Timothy 6:6-10*

God's law governs both our outward and our inward conduct, both our actions and our attitudes. Each area of life is important, and we must strive to please God with respect to each.

The more difficult to control are our inward attitudes. It is easier to refrain from murder than to keep from hating or being angry. It is easier to avoid adultery than to avoid lust. We can stifle a desire to boast, but the inner pride may remain. We can conquer all thoughts of stealing, but greed and covetousness may nevertheless dominate our lives.

While both aspects of our conduct are significant, we must learn to concentrate more upon developing the right inner attitudes. These are the more important, because what we are on the inside determines how we will act outwardly.

Why does a person murder? Because he has hatred or anger in his heart. What leads to adultery? Lust in the heart. Pride leads to boasting. A person steals because inwardly he is filled with greed or covetousness. As Jesus said, "For out of the heart proceed evil thoughts, murders, adulteries, fornications, thefts, false witness, blasphemies" (Matthew 15:19).

The last of the Ten Commandments focuses primarily upon the inward life. "Thou shalt not covet," it says.

Here God is telling us to have the right attitude toward things. Instead of being covetous, we must learn the grace of contentment. This is the basic principle underlying the last Commandment.

I. The Sin of Covetousness

Covetousness is a sin of the heart, a wrong attitude toward things. Basically, it is desire—the desire to acquire, possess, and use things. Now certainly not all desire is forbidden. Indeed, we are meant to desire and earnestly seek that which pertains to the kingdom of God. Also, it is not wrong to desire to get and accumulate goods and wealth as such.

Clearly the forbidden covetousness is a particular kind of desire, a sinful and unlawful desire to acquire and own a particular item. How can we tell the difference? How can we distinguish our lawful desires and aspirations from forbidden covetousness? How can we identify evil covetousness in our lives?

Wanting Forbidden Things

We know we are guilty of covetousness first of all if we find ourselves wanting forbidden things, i.e., things that belong to someone else or things to which we have no rightful claim.

The commandment specifically forbids harboring covetous desire for a neighbor's possessions. "Thou shalt not covet . . . any thing that is thy neighbor's" (Exodus 20:17). This is the sin of envy. It may involve not only the desire to possess a certain object, but also resentment toward the neighbor because he happens to have it, and we do not. In this case covetousness violates Christian love.

Covetousness may also be the desire to possess a thing that has been specifically forbidden by God. This was the sin that invaded Achan's heart after God had prohibited any looting of the city of Jericho by the conquering Israelite army (Joshua 6:17-19). As Achan himself told it, "When I saw among the spoils a goodly Babylonish garment, and two hundred shekels of silver, and a wedge of gold of fifty shekels weight, then I coveted them, and took them" (Joshua 7:21).

Covetousness may take the form of a "something-for-nothing" attitude, in which we desire to acquire a thing without expending any money or labor for it. Such an attitude is bound to result when honest labor is no longer seen as the primary means to ownership. In a give-away society characterized by indulgent parents, easy welfare, and ubiquitous sweepstakes, a Christian must work very hard to keep from becoming covetous.

Wanting Too Many Things

Covetousness may also take the form of wanting too many things, desiring to get more than we need, or can use. This is the sin of greed.

In their pursuit of unnecessary wealth many men and women have overwhelmed themselves in work; hence their family life and their church life have been sacrificed. Truly 1 Timothy 6:9 says, "But they that will be rich fall into temptation and a snare, and into many foolish and hurtful lusts, which drown men in destruction and perdition."

Worshiping Things

In its most basic form covetousness is the desire to acquire earthly possessions for their own sakes or for selfish reasons. 1 Timothy 6:10 calls it "the love of money." Colossians 3:5 identifies it as idolatry. Indeed, it is the worship of things, or setting one's affection on things on the earth (Colossians 3:2). Jesus calls it serving mammon (which means money) in the sense of making it a god (Matthew 6:24). It is the sin of materialism.

This worshipful attitude toward things is strongly condemned by Christ in Luke 12:13-21. Here He says to a family squabbling over an inheritance, "Take heed, and beware of covetousness: for a man's life consisteth not in the abundance of the things which he possesseth." He reinforces this warning by telling the story of the rich, foolish farmer who gloated over his wealth and put his trust in his earthly treasures. God wrought swift judgment upon him: "Thou fool, this night thy soul shall be required of thee." Then Jesus applies the judgment to covetous people everywhere: "So is he that layeth up treasure for himself, and is not rich toward God."

Here again we must emphasize that it is not things in themelves that are sinful, nor is the mere possession of things forbidden. It is the wrong attitude that is condemned, namely, the attitude of idolatrous attachment to, exclusive pursuit of, and foolish dependence upon things.

II. The Seriousness of Covetousness

Just how serious covetousness is can be seen from the account of Achan in Joshua 7. Here the sinister consequences of this sin are manifested to all.

First, covetousness is serious because it leads to all kinds of other sins. "For the love of money is the root of all evil: which while some coveted after, they have erred from the faith, and pierced themselves through with many sorrows" (1 Timothy 6:10).

In Achan's case covetousness led directly to theft and deceit (Joshua 7:21). For others it leads to armed robbery, prostitution, gambling, tax evasion, profaning the Lord's Day, neglect of parents, murder, or even warfare. The list is endless.

Covetousness is indeed a heart-sin; but if we harbor it in our hearts, it will sooner or later break forth into evil acts.

Another sad consequence of covetousness is that it hinders God's cause and kingdom. In the case of Achan, his disobedience led to the withdrawal of God's blessing and the subsequent defeat of the Israelites at Ai (Joshua 7:1-5).

Covetousness among Christians likewise hinders the advance of God's kingdom today. It robs God's church of the tithes and offerings needed for effective service in the areas of missions and benevolence. It robs the kingdom of many talented young men and women who choose vocations for the sake of money rather than ministry. It robs Christians of time they could be spending in local church work.

The seriousness of covetousness is seen finally in the severity with which it is condemned. In the case of Achan, both he and his family (who probably consented to what he did) were stoned to death, burned, and then covered with stones (Joshua 7:24-26).

God's Word is specific and severe: the covetous shall not enter the kingdom (1 Corinthians 6:10).

III. The Solution to Covetousness

God's solution to the attitude of covetousness is the development of another attitude, contentment. "But godliness with contentment is great gain. For we brought nothing into this world, and it is certain we can carry nothing out. And having food and raiment, let us be therewith content" (1 Timothy 6:6-8).

We must be like Paul, who said, "I have learned, in whatsoever state I am, therewith to be content" (Philippians 4:11).

12

The Greatest Commandment

Basic Scripture resources: Leviticus 19:18;
Deuteronomy 6:4, 5; Mark 12:28-34;
Luke 10:25-37; Romans 13:8-10

The Ten Commandments are a remarkably concise yet comprehensive code of conduct. But still this amazing list does not include the most important command of all: the command to *love.*

One day a man asked Jesus to single out the greatest of all the commandments. Probably he was expecting to hear one of the Ten Commandments named. But Jesus replied, "Thou shalt love the Lord thy God with all thy heart." Without waiting Jesus identified the second greatest command as also requiring love: "Thou shalt love thy neighbor as thyself" (Mark 12:30, 31; see Deuteronomy 6:5 and Leviticus 19:18).

I. Love and Law

There is considerable confusion regarding the proper relationship between love and law. Some are convinced that law is necessary only where people are still immature and unenlightened. After all, didn't Jesus himself usher in a new age in which law has supposedly been replaced by love? Are not we who are guided by love mature enough to discard rules and regulations? Since we have now come of age, surely we are capable of determining for ourselves what is the most loving course of action in each situation!

The above views are not at all rare in our time. In fact, the idea that love is able to replace the law is one of the central teachings of modern situation ethics. For instance, Joseph Fletcher, in his popular book, *Situation Ethics: The New Morality* (Philadelphia: Westminster Press, 1966), states categorically that Jesus and Paul replaced the precepts of law with the living principle of love (p. 69).

There are dangerous fallacies in this way of thinking. In the first place, Jesus did not do away with law. Concerning the law, Jesus said, "Do not think that I came to abolish the Law or the Prophets; I did not come to abolish, but to fulfill" (Matthew 5:17, NAS). Jesus did fulfill the parts of the Old Testament law that pointed forward to Him. For instance, the sin offerings of the Old Testament were types of Christ's death on the cross, and as such they were fulfilled and set aside when He went to Calvary. But the fact that Jesus set aside certain intentionally-temporary laws does not mean that He set aside law itself. The moral law is by its very own nature eternally valid, as we pointed out in chapter one.

In the second place, it is true that Jesus emphasized the commandment of love (John 15:12), but He never intended this commandment to replace all others. He never intended love to replace law. Love is but the condensation of the law; the various commandments simply spell out how to put love into action.

When Jesus specified the two greatest commands as the commands to love God and neighbor, He said, "On these two commandments depend the whole Law and the Prophets" (Matthew 22:40, NAS). That is, the love commandments support all the others. Every action or attitude demanded by God's spokesmen is but an expression of love. Love is *the* basic attitude from which all other virtues spring and of which all vices are a violation.

Love is simply the summary of the rest of God's law. The various commands embody the particular forms of love. They tell us what it means to love, or how a loving person acts. Love is like the trunk of a tree; the commands are the branches springing from it. Love is like a beautiful diamond; the commandments are its facets. One facet is "Be kind"; another facet is "Do not commit adultery." "Do not steal" means "Love does not steal." "Bear one another's burdens" means "Love bears another's burdens."

The apostle Paul leaves no doubt that love is the general attitude and the other commands are the particular expressions of it. Commenting specifically on neighbor-love, he says,

Owe nothing to anyone except to love one another; for he who loves his neighbor has fulfilled the law. For this, "You shall not commit adultery, You shall not murder, You shall not steal, You shall not covet," and if there is any other commandment, it is summed up in this saying, "You shall love your neighbor as yourself." Love does no wrong to a neighbor; love therefore is the fulfillment of the law (Romans 13:8-10, NAS).

Paul says in Galatians 5:14, "For the whole Law is fulfilled in one word, in the statement, 'You shall love your neighbor as yourself' " (NAS).

II. God's Love for Us

Since love is the greatest command of all, we should be very eager to know more about its nature. Just what is love? We can learn this by looking to the example and pattern for love, namely, God.

God is love (1 John 4:8). Jesus expressly commands us to imitate the way the Father expresses His love to all mankind. "Love your enemies . . . that ye may be the children of your Father which is in heaven. . . . Be ye therefore perfect, even as your Father which is in heaven is perfect" (Matthew 5:43-48; see 1 John 4:11).

God's love for mankind is a distinctive kind of love that the New Testament calls agape (pronounced ah-*gah*-pay). What is agape? Basically it is good will toward others. It is caring about them; it is a deep concern for their happiness and welfare. It is compassion upon those who are in need.

"God loves us" thus means that God is genuinely concerned for our well-being and happiness. God cares about us; He sees us in our need and has compassion upon us. The supreme evidence and demonstration of His love (concern, compassion) is Jesus Christ. Because God cares, He gave His only-begotten Son (John 3:16; 1 John 4:9).

Agape differs from other types of love in that it seeks to give and not to get. It seeks to satisfy not some need of the lover, but rather the needs of the one who is loved. This is clearly the case with God's love. He loves us not for what He can get out of us, but for what He can give to us.

Agape is unique because it is unconditional and universal. It is not based on some condition or quality in the one who is loved. It is not a matter of being attracted by the loveliness of a person. It is rather an overflowing concern directed to all people, even to the unloveliest and meanest.

This is truly how God loves. He is no respecter of persons; He does not favor some above others. "He maketh his sun to rise on the evil and on the good, and sendeth rain on the just and on the unjust" (Matthew 5:45). God does not love us because we earn His love with our good qualities; He loves us in spite of our ugliness. "But God commendeth his love toward us, in that, while we were yet sinners, Christ died for us" (Romans 5:8).

III. Our Love for God

Our supreme task is to love God. To know how much God loves us should make this task easier. As John says, "We love him, because he first loved us" (1 John 4:19).

Since this is the greatest commandment, we should be trying our very best to obey it. Yet how many of us actually, conscientiously seek to love God? How does one go about it? The following are some suggestions that should help us in our attempt to develop this most basic of all attitudes.

First, we must *think of God as a person.* Love is an interpersonal relationship. We cannot really love things; we can only love persons.

God is truly a person. He is all we think of in terms of personhood, and even more. It is wrong to think of God as some kind of animal or object, as many primitive people do. It is just as wrong to think of God as an impersonal force, as many modern "sophisticated" people do. God is a person who knows, thinks, wills, feels, and acts. Because He is a person, we can love Him.

(Actually God is *three* persons, known to us as Father, Son, and Holy Spirit, though the three are one God. See Matthew 28:19. The implications of this profound Biblical teaching will not be discussed here.)

Second, we must think of God *as a person who loves us.* Many pagan people have conceived of their gods as persons, but often as persons who have absolutely no love or concern for mankind. Such gods may be admired or feared, but it is difficult to love them. But let us remember that the true God is a person who *loves us.* The proof of this is Jesus Christ (John 3:16). To know that God loves us makes it easier for us to love Him (1 John 4:19).

Finally, we must think of God as a person *whom we want to please.* Agape-love is just this: caring about the other person, wanting to please him, wanting to make him happy, not wanting to hurt him. What hurts God? Our sin hurts Him; therefore if we love Him, we will want to avoid sin. What pleases Him? Our obedience pleases Him; therefore we should try our best to obey.

At this point we can see that love for God is basically two different things. First, it truly is a *commandment;* it is the law that summarizes and includes all other laws. Second, it is a *motive* for obeying all the other commandments of God. As Jesus said in John 14:15, "If you love Me, you will keep My commandments" (NAS). See also 1 John 5:3.

As Christians we must continually strive to increase our conscious efforts to love God. To this end we must meditate more upon Him and His love for us. We must think more about what He has done for us out of His great love. We must try to be more aware of His immediate, personal presence within us.

13

Love in Action

Basic Scripture resources: Mark 2:13-17;
Luke 15:11-32; 1 Corinthians 9:19-23;
Galatians 5:25—6:5

Loving God cannot be separated from love for neighbors. This is why Jesus specified neighbor-love as the second greatest commandment without even waiting to be asked. As 1 John 4:20, 21 says,

> If some one says, "I love God," and hates his brother, he is a liar; for the one who does not love his brother whom he has seen, cannot love God whom he has not seen. And this commandment we have from Him, that the one who loves God should love his brother also (NAS).

Neighbor-love must be agape. That is, it must follow the pattern of God's love for us. We must love all people, just as God does. This includes our family, our neighbors, our friends, and even our enemies. How can we do this? We must remember that the essence of agape is *caring* about them. We do not have to like someone (i.e., be attracted to him) in order to love him. This is the presupposition of the missionary enterprise; we *care* about people in other parts of the world, even though we have never met them.

Christian love, then, is having a genuine concern for the happiness and welfare of all people, the lovely and the unlovely alike.

Most of all we need to remember that Christian love is *active,* not passive. It cannot remain hidden in the heart. It compels us to act. It demands concrete expression. As 1 John 3:18 says, "Little children, let us not love with word or with tongue, but in deed and truth" (NAS).

In this chapter we shall consider several different ways in which we must express our love for one another.

I. Love Compels Us to Bear Burdens

One way in which loving concern finds expression is through bearing the burdens of others. "Bear ye one another's burdens, and so fulfil the law of Christ," says Galatians 6:2. The law of Christ, of course, is that we love one another (John 15:12).

The particular kind of burdens that Paul has in mind here is spiritual burdens, or problems of the spiritual life. This is seen in the immediately preceding verse, Galatians 6:1, which says, "Brethren, if a man be overtaken in a fault, ye which are spiritual, restore such a one in the spirit of meekness. . . ."

Such a command is difficult to obey in a society where independence and self-reliance are held in such high esteem. Because of our fierce pride we are reluctant to admit our spiritual weakness and failures to others. Anyone who tries to be helpful in this respect is accused of being nosy and is often told to mind his own business!

But the very nature of Christian love and fellowship is that we must care when a brother or sister in Christ is having spiritual difficulty. We must not ignore him, or gossip about him, or condemn him, or ridicule him, or scorn him. We should want to give him strength and encouragement in fighting and striving against sin, and we should gently rebuke him for his sins and lovingly lead him to repentance.

James 5:19, 20 says, "Brethren, if any of you do err from the truth, and one convert him; let him know, that he which converteth the sinner from the error of his way shall save a soul from death, and shall hide a multitude of sins."

Sometimes this may be very difficult, and we may not like to do it. But love compels such burdenbearing. Romans 15:1, 2 exhorts, "We then that are strong ought to bear the infirmities of the weak, and not to please ourselves. Let every one of us please his neighbor for his good to edification."

The church must be like a stone arch, with each Christian helping to support all the others, and Christ the keystone upholding all.

II. Love Compels Us to Forgive

The real test of love is when someone sins against us. We may be very generous and sympathetic toward one whose sin does not cause us harm. But how do we react when we personally have been slandered or mistreated or cheated?

If we can respond in such a situation not by seeking to get even but with a spirit of forgiveness, then we know that we love our neighbors. For as we know, neighbor-love must include not only our friends and brethren, but also our enemies (Matthew 5:44).

The Prodigal's Father

In the parable of the prodigal son (Luke 15:11-32) Jesus shows how love is expressed in forgiveness in the person of the prodigal's father.

The prodigal son had indeed sinned grievously against his father. He had spurned his father's love, abandoned his responsibility on his father's farm, wasted his portion of the father's estate, scorned his father's moral teaching, and exhibited a general disrespect for his patient parent.

But how does the father respond to his son's pitiful, repentant request to be received back into just the outer fringes of the household? He does nothing less than restore him to the full rights and privileges of sonship, giving him gifts and calling for festive rejoicing. He does not accuse or condemn; he does not even mention his son's sins. Because he loves, he forgives.

The Heavenly Father

The father in this parable, of course, represents our heavenly Father, who is the supreme example of the kind of love that compels one to forgive. As in the parable, His love and forgiveness are not just empty words but are demonstrated by His actions. He has done everything in His power to make forgiveness a reality for each of us. "But God commendeth his love toward us, in that, while we were yet sinners, Christ died for us" (Romans 5:8).

We must respond in the same way to our enemies, to those who have sinned against us. We must forgive them and let them know that we have forgiven them. Concerning such a one who has sinned against the whole church, Paul says that we must "forgive him, and comfort him, lest perhaps such a one should be swallowed up with overmuch sorrow. Wherefore I beseech you that ye would confirm your love toward him" (2 Corinthians 2:7, 8).

III. Love Compels Us to Seek the Lost

The most authentic expression of love is evangelism. If we really care about the welfare of others, our greatest concern will be for their eternal destiny. There is something artificial about a love that acts to relieve the physical discomforts of this life for others, and yet does nothing to save them from the eternal torments of hell.

In our day two themes are constantly being emphasized: love (e.g., "make love, not war"), and "doing your own thing." But these two things are contradictory. If we really love one another, we must sacrifice "doing our own thing" (i.e., doing what pleases us) in order to reach the lost where they are.

Jesus Sought Sinners

The greatest example of such a self-denying love is, of course, Jesus Christ. His love for sinners led Him to do whatever He could to bring them to repentance. He himself was completely sinless and hated sin with a holy passion. Yet He did not shun sinners and try to avoid contact with them. In fact, He associated with them whenever He could. He ate and drank with those who were considered outcasts by the self-righteous "religious" people of His time (Mark 2:13-17).

Jesus did not do this because He enjoyed the company of sinners and sought fellowship with them. He did have godly friends, such as Lazarus and his sisters, Mary and Martha; and He occasionally visited with them and had fellowship with them. But more often than not He sacrificed pleasant hours with them in order to seek the lost. As He said, "They that are whole have no need of the physician, but they that are sick: I came not to call the righteous, but sinners to repentance" (Mark 2:17).

All Things to All Men

The apostle Paul has also shown us how real love seeks the lost. He did not wait for people to come to him; he went to them. He identified with their situation as much as possible (without compromising his Christian principles, of course) in order to get next to their hearts.

Paul describes his self-denying love for us in 1 Corinthians 9:19-22. Here he says,

For though I be free from all men, yet have I made myself servant unto all, that I might gain the more. And unto the Jews I became as a Jew, that I might gain the Jews; to them that are under the law, as under the law, that I might gain them that are under the law; to them that are without law, as without law, (being not without law to God, but under the law to Christ,) that I might gain them that are without law. To the weak became I as weak, that I might gain the weak: I am made all things to all men, that I might by all means save some.

Love does not do that which merely is convenient. Until we have gone out of our way to call sinners to repentance, until we have made ourselves servants to all in order to win some, we cannot claim to love.

14

The Highest Good

Basic Scripture resources: Psalm 119:97-106;
Matthew 5:14-16; 6:1-6, 25-34;
1 Corinthians 10:31

Thus far in this series of lessons we have been concerned with *knowing* God's will as He has revealed it to us in His law. It has been taken for granted that we are also concerned with *doing* God's will once we learn what it is. In other words, it is assumed that we truly want to obey God's commands.

This leads us to a question that philosophers and thinkers have discussed for literally thousands of years, namely, the question of the "highest good." It can be simply stated in this way: what is the most important thing we can hope to accomplish by our acts and deeds?

When we stop to think about it, we realize that our actions are usually not ends in themselves but are the *means* of bringing about some higher end or goal. For instance, when we take a drink of water, we don't do it just for the sake of drinking. We do it for a purpose, probably to quench our thirst. But even the quenching of thirst is a means to a still higher goal, such as the relief of discomfort or the attaining of a feeling of well-being. Some may say that even the attaining of well-being is but a means of being freed from creaturely distractions so that we can concentrate on the highest goal of all, namely, bringing honor and glory to God.

This sequence of purposes applies to *everything* we do, whether we are conscious of it or not. We have a purpose we are trying to achieve, a goal we are striving to attain. By our actions, including our acts of obedience to God's law, we are working to bring about a particular end result.

In this final chapter we want to do two things. First, we want to learn from the Word of God just what the most important goal in life *should* be. We will do this through a study of Matthew 6:33. Second, we want honestly to examine our own lives to see if we are indeed seeking that goal.

I. The Goal

In Matthew 6:33 Jesus says, "But seek first His kingdom, and His righteousness; and all these things shall be added to you" (NAS). In the first part of this statement our Lord tells us specifically what the highest good or ultimate goal in life should be: the kingdom of God.

When Jesus says, "Seek first," He is informing us that one's life should and does have an ultimate purpose. Without doubt many people have no conscious goal in life. They are aimless and drifting; they have "dropped out." But Jesus says "Seek!" He commands us to have a target, to be looking for something, to be trying to accomplish something. This forces us to stop and ask ourselves, "Just what *do* I want out of life? Just what am I trying to achieve?"

Someone may try to avoid the question by saying, "I'm interested in lots of things. I don't have just *one* goal." But he does have one supreme goal, even if he has not stopped to think about it. For each person there will always be one thing that is more important than all others—one thing that means more to him than anything else—one thing that he wants above all else.

To many people (perhaps the majority), the most important thing in life is personal pleasure or happiness. Their rule is to do only those things that bring about a freedom from pain (including anxiety) and a sense of well-being. As one rock singer said, "I believe . . . that the whole idea down here on the old earth is to be happy. . . . You have to enjoy what time you have, and it's fairly short." A literary critic put it this way: "To me, pleasure and my own personal happiness . . . are all I deem worth a hoot. . . . I have all that I can do to look out for my own happiness and welfare."

Happiness, of course, is relative. One person may not be satisifed until he has achieved considerable fame and fortune. Another may be satisfied with comparatively little. A "man-on-the-street" interviewer asked various people to state their concept of the "good life." One person replied,

> To me the good life would simply be a steady job and the income to the point where I'm not wealthy, just comfortable. I have a few meager material things I'd want, such as a good record player and records—things dealing with music. Dependable transportation. And a place to live. And a little money on the side in case I need it, a couple of hundred, even, in the bank, and enough spare change in my pocket so that when I run out of cigarettes I can buy them with the money I got in my pocket.

The ultimate parody of such materialistic hedonism comes from a Burger Chef place mat. It pictures a quarter-pound hamburger sandwich and describes its contents: juicy beef, cheese, lettuce, tomatoes, pickles, onions, and scrumptious sauce. Then it concludes, "Everything that makes life worth living on a golden sesame seed bun!"

At least the people in these examples *know* what they are seeking out of life. Tragically, however, they are seeking the wrong thing. Jesus not only commands us to be conscious of our goal; He also tells us what that goal must be, namely, the kingdom of God.

The word *kingdom* sometimes means the realm over which a king reigns. Its more basic meaning, though, is the king's reign or kingship itself. Other synonyms are lordship, power, glory, and honor. This is its meaning in Matthew 6:33. Thus when Jesus says, "Seek first His kingdom," He is saying that we must be seeking God's kingship and glory above all else. In other words, the most important thing in all the world is to bring honor and glory to God. "Whether, then, you eat or drink or whatever you do, do all to the glory of God" (1 Corinthians 10:31, NAS).

The basic difference between Jesus' teaching and the view described above is this: do you do what you do simply to please yourself, or do you do it to please and honor God? The following contrast illustrates the difference. George Foster, a baseball superstar, has been interviewed many times after an outstanding performance. In his comments he seldom forgets to praise God for his talents. Manifesting a different attitude is Mack Wilken, champion Olympic discus thrower. After he won this event in a recent Olympics, a reporter asked him whether he did it for himself or for his country. His reply was something like this: "I did it for myself. If the U.S. wants to try to claim some of the glory, let it go ahead. But I did it for myself."

How about you? Do you live and act only to please yourself, or to please and honor God first of all?

II. The Means

The next item to be discussed is the *means* of achieving our goal. We seek to honor God above all else. What is the best way to do this? Jesus gives the answer in Matthew 6:33 in the words "and His righ-teousness." Nothing enhances and magnifies the lordship of God quite as much as does the effort to conform our lives to the righteousness of God.

The expression "God's righteousness" can mean different things in different contexts. Here it most likely refers to His righteous and holy will as ex-pressed in His commandments. Thus it refers to our efforts to obey His will and live pure and righteous lives. Indeed, righteous living—being good and doing good—is truly the best means of honoring God.

This is the meaning of Jesus' statement in Matthew 5:16: "Let your light shine before men in such a way that they may see your good works, and glorify your Father who is in heaven" (NAS). It is possible for us to do good works in a way that glorifies ourselves, so that others will notice us and honor us. Jesus calls this hypocrisy and condemns it (Matthew 6:1-6).

On the other hand, it is possible to use our righteous deeds as spotlights directing people toward God, when we give Him all the glory and praise. An example of this is the great change in Paul's life following his conversion. Certainly the Christians marveled that their former enemy was now preaching and serving Christ. But Paul did not use his conversion and his preaching just to soak up their admiration. His whole life was pointed toward God, so that he could say of those who knew him, "And they were glorifying God because of me" (Galatians 1:24, NAS).

We should remember that the reverse is true as well. Our righteous deeds do indeed honor God; but when we who wear his name do evil deeds, this actually brings *dishonor* upon Him. Paul warns us of this in Romans 2:23, 24: "You who boast in the Law, through your breaking the Law, do you dishonor God? For 'the name of God is blasphemed among the Gentiles be-cause of you,' just as it is written" (NAS).

When a person is known as a Christian, it is as if he had this message printed on every T-shirt and jacket: "I am a Christian. I represent the God of our Lord Jesus Christ. Whatever you see me doing shows you what I think of my God."

All of us must ask ourselves, "Am I doing the things that bring honor to my Lord? Or does my conduct bring disgrace and shame upon His name? Even when we are doing things that are righteous in themselves, we must ask, "Am I doing this for the right reason? Am I obeying God because I know it pleases Him and glorifies Him, or am I doing it for some selfish reason?"

There are a number of important lessons connected with this point. One lesson is that being good is not an end in itself; there is something much more important at stake. Another lesson is that *doing what is right* is the most important thing in the world we can *do,* because this is our best way of glorifying God. A final lesson is that we can do right things for the wrong reasons and thus dishonor and displease God. For instance, being good in order to be saved (or to go to Heaven) is missing the mark. We are saved by grace through faith; we do good works to honor and please the God we love.

III. The Result

In Matthew 6:33 Jesus makes a very significant promise. He says that if you seek first God's kingdom and righteousness, "all these things shall be added to you." The *result* of putting God's kingdom first is that God will provide the very things most people seem to be panting after. When we devote ourselves to serving God, the provisions for our worldly needs will be supplied as a kind of byproduct or serendipity.

What are "all these things" that God promises to supply? The context shows that Jesus is talking about the daily necessities of life, such as food and clothing—in other words, the things that contribute to the material comfort and happiness of life. This is apparent in Matthew 6:25, 31, 32 as Jesus says,

> For this reason I say to you, do not be anxious for your life, as to what you shall eat, or what you shall drink; nor for your body, as to what you shall put on. Is not life more than food, and the body than clothing? . . . Do not be anxious then, saying, "What shall we eat?" or "What shall we drink?" or "With what shall we clothe ourselves?" For all these things the Gentiles eagerly seek; for your heavenly Father knows that you need all these things.

How tragic it is that those who *seek* happiness, those who make it their actual *goal* in life, usually do not find it. The secret of happiness is not to seek after it, but to strive to honor God and just trust His promise that He will give us what we need. Could we ask for greater peace of mind or freedom from worry than this?

This little book has only scratched the surface in the study of God's commandments. We could study and meditate upon them for the rest of our days without exhausting their implications for our lives. Indeed, may we *want* to do so! May we have the loving dedication and devotion of the psalmist who says in Psalm 119:97,

> O how I love Thy law!
> It is my meditation all the day (NAS).

But we can never be content just to *know* God's law. We must resolve to obey it and to conform our lives to it, as Psalm 119:105-106 says,

Thy word is a lamp to my feet,
And a light to my path.
I have sworn, and I will confirm it,
That I will keep Thy righteous ordinances (NAS).

Why will we keep them? Above all else, to honor and please our gracious lawgiver himself.